START YOUR OWN

LAWN CARE OR LANDSCAPING BUSINESS

Additional titles in **Entrepreneur's Startup Series**

Start Your Own

Arts and Crafts Business

Automobile Detailing Business

Bar and Club

Bed and Breakfast

Blogging Business

Business on eBay

Car Wash

Child-Care Service

Cleaning Service

Clothing Store and More

Coaching Business

Coin-Operated Laundry

College Planning Consultant Business

Construction and Contracting Business

Consulting Business

Day Spa and More

eBusiness

eLearning or Training Business

Event Planning Business

Executive Recruiting Business

Fashion Accessories Business

Florist Shop and Other Floral Businesses

Food Truck Business

Freelance Writing Business and More

Freight Brokerage Business

Gift Basket Business and More

Grant-Writing Business

Graphic Design Business

Green Business

Hair Salon and Day Spa

Home Inspection Service

Import/Export Business

Information Marketing Business

Kid-Focused Business

Lawn Care or Landscaping Business

Mail Order Business

Medical Claims Billing Service

Microbrewery, Distillery, or Cidery

Net Services Business

Nonprofit Organization

Online Coupon or Daily Deal Business

Online Education Business

Personal Concierge Service

Personal Training Business

Pet Business and More

Pet-Sitting Business and More

Photography Business

Public Relations Business

Restaurant and More

Retail Business and More

Self-Publishing Business

Seminar Production Business

Senior Services Business

Specialty Food Businesses

Staffing Service

Transportation Service

Travel Business and More

Tutoring and Test Prep Business

Vending Business

Wedding Consultant Business

Wholesale Distribution Business

Entrepreneur
MAGAZINE'S

 STARTUP

START YOUR OWN

LAWN CARE OR LANDSCAPING BUSINESS

Fourth Edition

YOUR STEP-BY-STEP GUIDE TO SUCCESS

The Staff of Entrepreneur Media, Inc. & Cheryl Kimball

Entrepreneur
PRESS®

Entrepreneur Press, Publisher
Cover Design: Andrew Welyczko
Production and Composition: Eliot House Productions

This publication is designed to provide accurate and authoritative information in regard to the
subject matter covered. It is sold with the understanding that the publisher is not engaged in
rendering legal, accounting or other professional services. If legal advice or other expert assistance
is required, the services of a competent professional person should be sought.

Library of Congress Cataloging-in-Publication Data
Names: Kimball, Cheryl. | Entrepreneur Media, Inc.
Title: Start your own lawn care or landscaping business: your step-by-step guide to success/by the
    staff of Entrepreneur Media, Inc., and Cheryl Kimball.
Description: Irvine, California : Entrepreneur Media, Inc., 2016. | Revision of: Third edition /
    Entrepreneur Press and Ciree Linsenmann. 2011. | Includes index.
Identifiers: LCCN 2016014320| ISBN 978-1-59918-592-7 (alk. paper) | ISBN 1-59918-592-X
    (alk. paper)
Subjects: LCSH: Lawn care industry—Management. | Landscaping industry—Management. | Small
    business. | New business enterprises.
Classification: LCC SB433.27 .L56 2016 | DDC 635.9/647068—dc23
LC record available at https://lccn.loc.gov/2016014320

Printed in the United States of America

20 19 18 17 16   10 9 8 7 6 5 4 3 2 1

Contents

Chapter 6
Cutting-Edge Help **73**

Chapter 7
Tools of the Trade **83**

Preface

From 2000-2011, the number of non-farm proprietors grew by 10.7 million—far exceeding government or private employment, the latter of which actually declined by 1.26 million during that same period (www.newgeography.com). Self-employment and business ownership clearly continues to be a preferred means of wage earning.

Whether you're ready for a career change, are tired of working for someone else, or just interested in making a few extra bucks every month, a lawn care service business is a viable way to achieve your goal. There's plenty of work for even a new business owner in most parts of the country. The initial investment in equipment and the monthly overhead is fairly low. Plus the pay is great—and you get lots of fresh air and exercise while you earn it.

While this book contains all the advice and tips you need to be successful in the green game, you won't get instructions here on how to mow lawns, sculpt magnificent topiaries, or winterize your weed whacker. Those are basic skills you need to develop on your own—either by practicing on unsuspecting clients' lawns or by studying turf grass basics at your local community college. What you will get, however, is a solid background in what it takes to run a successful business. Although you may not realize it now, you need to be a pretty shrewd businessperson in addition to a mowing maven to make this whole gig work.

For instance, you have to know how and where to find new clients because clients = work = taxable income (which will of course be of particular interest to Uncle Sam). You have to know how to balance your books and develop sideline businesses to keep yourself busy when the snow gets too deep to trim the rose bushes. And you have to know enough about turf and weather conditions in your part of the country to become a true Grass Master.

Here's a sampling of the major topics covered in this book:

▶ Estimating lawn size and setting your price
▶ Deciding which lawn care services to offer
▶ Determining who and where your best customers are and how to market to them
▶ Setting up a viable business structure and naming your fledgling business
▶ Writing a business plan (and you thought all you needed was a riding mower and good weather!)
▶ Finding the right business professionals to advise you
▶ Selecting the right lawn maintenance equipment, vehicles, and supplies
▶ Hiring employees as your business grows
▶ Learning from industry gurus, trade associations, and other sources
▶ How to reflect current turf industry trends through your business practices
▶ Conquering the mysteries of the internet and harnessing its power to grow your business
▶ Determining the cost of doing business and managing your finances

You'll also find stories and advice here from successful lawn care business owners from around the country that can help give you the confidence you'll need to make your fledgling business work.

Does this sound like just the job for you? Then, gentlemen and ladies alike, start your engines and let the mowing begin!

The Green, Green Grass of Home

When you think back to the long, lazy summers of your youth, chances are your recollections are full of achingly nostalgic memories. Picture an oversized tire swing under a big, shady tree and tall, frosty glasses of lemonade wreathed in pearls of moisture. In the background the high-pitched whine of lawn mowers drone. If you're like a lot of people, you were trudging along behind one of those mowers back then, pushing with all your might and sweating profusely, just so you could make a few bucks to buy some baseball cards or a really cool bike. You may have occasionally mowed down a few pansies or zebra-striped a lawn, but you sure were proud when the homeowner came to the door, surveyed your handiwork, and forked over the agreed-upon fee.

Mowing lawns or landscaping residential or commercial properties for a living can give you that same sense of pride—while earning you some pretty serious cash.

The Green Scene

There are many advantages to running a homebased lawn care or landscaping service. You're master of your own destiny, and can devote as much or little time to the business as you want. You have a short commute to work if you're based in your own community and can work at your own pace at virtually any time during regular daylight hours. You also can enjoy the fresh air, get a good cardiovascular workout, and bulk up your muscles.

The price of all this freedom and body contouring is relatively low—so low, in fact, that many new lawn service owners and landscapers use their personal credit cards or small personal loans to fund their new businesses. Once you invest in the tools and toys you need to manicure lawns or install landscaping professionally, you're generally set for years. You don't need much in the way of office equipment, either, and you can set your office up in a corner of the den or a spare bedroom rather than laying out extra cash for a commercial space.

Reality Check

This all sounds pretty appealing, doesn't it? But of course, every Garden of Eden has a serpent, and lawn care and landscaping businesses have quite a few of their own coiled and waiting to strike. To begin, you have to be a lot more adept at mowing, trimming, and pruning than the average person. That means you'll have to invest some time in learning gardening basics and techniques. You'll have to be a disciplined self-starter who can ignore the call of a glorious spring day and diligently service your clients rather than heading for the lake or golf course. You have to be physically fit and able to handle the rigors of the job, which can include lifting heavy equipment off and onto trailers, and wielding bulky handheld implements for hours at a time. You'll be handling potentially dangerous machinery and hazardous chemicals. You'll also have to be a very savvy business manager who can administer cash flow, create advertising and marketing campaigns, and implement a survival plan that will take you through the lean winter months.

► Do You Have the Right Stuff?

Ask yourself these questions to see if you have what it takes to become a successful lawn service owner:

- ► Am I motivated enough to work without a bear of a boss breathing down my neck? ___
- ► Can I resist driving my sit-down mower over to the park for some R&R on beautiful summer days? ___
- ► Do I have the stamina and commitment to slather on sunblock regularly and spend a lot of time wrestling with flowering trees in gigantic pots under the blazing sun? ___
- ► Can I train my computer mouse to click on "Landscape Illustrator 5.0" when it really wants to go play in "Final Fantasy XV: Episode Duscae"? ___
- ► Can I tell the difference between turf and Astroturf in a blindfold test? ___
- ► Can I develop a viable sideline business to support any unbreakable habits I may have (e.g., paying the mortgage, buying groceries, etc.) during the winter? ___
- ► Am I willing to keep myself informed on the latest in lawn care trends? ___
- ► Can I keep my four-year-old from answering my business telephone line with, "Hi, can you come over and play?" during working hours? ___
- ► Am I willing to wear a personalized company T-shirt in colors that blend tastefully with my landscaping equipment? ___
- ► Am I willing to work long hours in the hope of earning big bucks? ___

Total your "yes" answers. Scoring:

8–10	=	Congratulations! You are truly the Blade Master.
4–7	=	The force is with you. Work hard and prosper.
1–3	=	It's a good thing you bought this book.
0	=	Maybe you should try a career in floral design or culinary arts instead.

Even with such obstacles, it is possible to prosper in this industry. In the chapters ahead, we'll show you how to lay the groundwork to start a thriving lawn care service or landscaping business. We'll cover day-to-day responsibilities and the various tasks integral to running this type of business. We'll also touch on the myriad issues a new business owner will face, such as tax, insurance, and financing matters. Perhaps best of all, we'll share advice from successful lawn care and landscaping business owners who have made their personal dreams of prospering in a business they love come true.

What we won't do in this book is teach you how to mow or fertilize or design landscapes. That type of teaching is best left to the pros. Rather, we'll give you all the insight you need to set up your business in a way that will give you the best chance for success.

Industry Snapshot

Before we get into the nitty-gritty of running a professional lawn care or landscaping business, let's take a look at the green industry as a whole and the opportunities it presents for aspiring entrepreneurs like you.

According to the National Association of Landscape Professionals (NALP, formerly PLANET at www.landscapeprofessionals.org), 80 percent of the contractors surveyed for the "Landscape Management Industry Pulse Report 2014" described the state of the market as "very healthy" compared to just 56 percent just two years earlier in 2012. What may be even more promising is that a survey conducted by the Harris Poll for the NALP found that 67 percent of Americans in the survey agree that "professional landscape help would allow them to have a nicer yard."

What is known for sure, according to the *Occupational Outlook Handbook*, 2014–16 edition (U.S. Department of Labor, Bureau of Labor Statistics—www. bls.gov), is that "more workers will be needed to keep up with the increasing demand for lawn care, landscaping, and cleaning services from large institutions, including universities and corporate campuses."

The market they serve is huge. In 2015, the market size of the landscaping services industry was $76 billion, according to IBISWorld's (www.ibisworld.com) report "Landscaping Services in the U.S." (NAICS, November 2015) with an annual growth expectation of 3.3 percent through 2020. According to Recruiter (www.recruiter. com), demand for tree trimmers and pruners, for example, is supposed to continue upward over the next

tip

"Grasscycling" (the act of leaving lawn clippings on the lawn after mowing) encourages a healthier lawn by returning nutrients to the soil in a slow-release manner. Mowing a dry lawn with sharp blades and removing no more than one-third of the leaf blade at each cutting encourages the grasscycling process. For more tips, visit the University of Maryland Extension's Home and Garden Information Center (https://extension.umd. edu/hgic).

few years with a predicted annual increase of 6.41 percent in new jobs. Sharpen up those tools, tree trimmers!

Who's driving this industry? The nearly 76 million aging baby boomers, many of whom are affluent homeowners. They recognize the value of a well-kept lawn and beautifully designed and landscaped yard, but they often don't have the time or the inclination to do the maintenance themselves.

Of course, baby boomers aren't the only ones who go online or look in the phone book to find a reputable lawn or landscape professional. Other potential customers for landscaping include:

stat fact

According to the Green Industry Pros Industry (www.greenindustrypros. com) Business Report, "Roughly 60 percent of [equipment] suppliers said both equipment and parts business was up [in 2014], while 55 percent said they also saw an increase in service business."

▶ Homeowners who don't have the vision, skill, or tools to design their own landscaping

▶ New homeowners who wish to update their existing landscaping

▶ Homeowners who plan to put their homes on the market and want to improve curb appeal with fresh or updated landscaping

▶ Builders of both residential and commercial properties who don't already have their own landscapers on staff

Potential customers for lawn maintenance include:

▶ Homeowners who are frequently out of town on business

▶ Retirees who don't care to do their own maintenance any longer

▶ "Snowbirds" with winter homes in warmer climates

▶ Golf course managers who may need help with maintenance

▶ Rental property or condominium association managers who are personnel-impaired

▶ Facilities managers for botanical gardens, historic buildings, municipalities and other government entities, universities, cemeteries, and other public places with green spaces

Some of these commercial contracts may already be spoken for by an on-staff, veteran landscaper, but let's face it, you never know when an opportunity may arise, either because a potential client is not happy with the service he or she has been receiving or because someone retires or leaves an organization. Timing is everything, so keep connecting with potential new opportunities.

Later in this book, we'll discuss the various ways you can market your services so you're in the right place at the right time when an opportunity pops up. Then, by offering the right mix of services, you'll be able to clip off a neat little piece of this business yourself.

Exactly how much can you earn? The sky's truly the limit. The lawn care and landscaping business owners we interviewed for this book earned anywhere from $5,000 to $50,000 in their first year, and as much as $160,000 to $280,000 once they were in business a few years. They offer services ranging from basic mowing and trimming to landscape design, installation and maintenance, xeriscape renovation, natural pest control and fertilizing, and chemical application.

The Bureau of Labor Statistics' May 2014 industry-specific wage estimates show average wages for landscaping-related jobs as follows: landscaping and groundskeeping workers, $26,190; grounds maintenance workers, $26,890; pest control workers, $32,690; pesticide handlers, $32,950; tree trimmers/pruners, $33,880.

stat fact

"Landscaping product demand is forecast to grow 5.3 percent per year, from $5.3 billion in 2014 to $8.2 billion in 2019, as the market continues to recover from the effects of the 2007–2009 recession. Hardscape unit demand outpaces overall landscape product business."

—*Concrete News* 8/24/15

Types of Green Industry Service Businesses

There are numerous ways to get into the lawn and landscaping industry. The basic types of lawn and landscaping businesses include:

▶ Lawn mowing/maintenance
▶ Sod installation/hydroseeding
▶ Weeding or fertilizer and/or pest control application
▶ Landscape care/maintenance services
▶ Landscape design/contracting services
▶ Landscape architecture services

We'll discuss these types of businesses and the services they typically offer, as well as a few others, in the respective lawn and landscaping chapters. In the meantime, it's important to note that while many entrepreneurs choose to specialize in a particular type of service, it's also not unusual for a business owner to offer a selection of complementary services. For example, landscape maintenance companies also may offer irrigation services (lawn sprinklers, fountains, etc.), in addition to trimming, mulching, and other common landscaping services. Or lawn service business owners may choose to offer snow removal services during the winter as a way to generate an income year-round.

Other Opportunities to Get Green

Although we are assuming for the purposes of this book that you are planning to start your own lawn and/or landscaping business from the ground up, it's worth mentioning that there are a number of green industry franchises that can help you establish your own business. There are turnkey operations for lawn and landscaping, irrigation, deck construction, concrete installation, and many other green industry-related businesses, all of which can require a fairly substantial capital investment. We've listed contact information for some of them under "Franchise Opportunities" in the Appendix in case you'd like to check them out.

Meet the Entrepreneurs

A number of lawn care and landscaping business owners graciously agreed to be interviewed for this book to give you a true insider's view of the industry:

- ▶ *Nathan Bowers* is the owner of Premier Lawn Services, Inc., in Sykesville, Maryland. Although he founded the business in 1990, he has been involved in grounds maintenance services since he was 14, when "Dad handed me the Craftsman hand mower and said, 'Why don't you go make a few bucks mowing the neighbor's lawn?'" Bowers says. He attended college for a few years before deciding to make lawn care his full-time job.
- ▶ *Michael Collins and Karen Deighton* are owners of Celtic Lawn & Landscape, LLC, which was established in Livonia, Michigan, in 2005. This mother-and-son-in-law duo bring different skills to the cutting table, so to speak—Collins is the lawn/landscape/snow-meister, while Deighton handles the administrative side. He

tip

Xeriscaping is the purposeful use of native plants to create drought-tolerant landscapes and lower or eliminate the need for watering. It is preferred by conservation-minded homeowners. Desert and dry regions with water restrictions offer xeriscape resources to their citizens through county-sponsored councils, including water-saving landscape tips, design ideas, and xeriscape landscaper listings. Search for a xeriscape council in your area if you'd like to cash in on this part of the market. Visit Colorado's version here: www.coloradowaterwise.org/xeriscapecolorado.

earned a degree in business administration in workforce management from the University of Michigan-Dearborn and most recently was a human resources generalist, although he did lawn and landscape work while in college. Deighton received a bachelor's degree in mathematics from Madonna University in Livonia, Michigan, and works full time as a controller for a construction company.

▶ *Steve Mager* has been the owner of The Cutting Crew in Mendota Heights, Minnesota, since 1998. He offers chemical services in addition to lawn maintenance for commercial and residential accounts. He holds a bachelor's degree in education from St. Cloud State University in St. Cloud, Minnesota, and previously was a property maintenance supervisor for a company that managed 30 residential group homes for the mentally disabled.

▶ *Lowell Pitser* is the owner of Lowell's Lawn Service in Stanwood, Washington. He previously worked as a land surveyor and literally fell into lawn maintenance as a career—he sustained a bad fall on the job that hurt his back, so on the advice of his doctor, he sought new employment. Because he couldn't even push his hand mower anymore, he borrowed a riding lawn mower one day to cut his own lawn, and within the hour was approached by a couple of neighbors who asked if he could do their lawns, too. "Every time I'd mow, someone else would ask if I could do his lawn, too, and I realized there could be a lot of money in this field," he says. And he was right—he had 35 customers the first year and eventually added an employee to help with the business.

▶ *Kelly Giard* is the owner of Clean Air Lawn Care in Fort Collins, Colorado. In 2006 Kelly began what is now the nation's leading sustainable lawn care service. His MA in economics and BA in environmental politics and analysis, courtesy of Boston University, sure didn't hurt when he decided to trade in his stockbroker career and put on the green cape. In 2008 he teamed up with friends and his wife, Stephanie Giard, to turn this innovative business into a franchise opportunity for the environmentally friendly, hungry entrepreneur. The solar panels on his truck that charge the whisper-soft mowers attract a lot of attention for this unique professional who has a different way of doing things.

▶ *Mike Rosenbleeth* is the Niceville, Florida, owner of Grass Roots Lawn & Landscape, Inc. After retiring twice, once from a 20-year career in the U.S. Air Force, where he earned the rank of captain, and then from a ten-year second career with a defense contractor, Rosenbleeth started his green business in 2002 because he wanted to do something as different as possible from his previous jobs. In addition to a bachelor's degree in aerospace engineering from Texas A&M University, he holds a master's degree in aeronautical engineering from the Air Force Institute of Technology at Wright-Patterson Air Force Base in Dayton, Ohio.

► *Marc Wise's* degree in environmental studies from Prescott College in Arizona helped him turn his entrepreneurial desires into reality. Prescott's special program coaches students for niche creation within the environmental industry. After several years working first as a chiropractor and then as a laborer for an organic lawn care business in Ohio, Marc's experience led him to develop and grow Greenwise Organic Lawncare in Evanstan, Illinois, with his partner, Lindsay Stame. Lindsay brought critical managerial and business administration skills to the table with her degree in communications from Northwestern University in Illinois and experience in the banking industry.

tip

Do your part to be environmentally friendly by recycling both used nursery containers (which are usually made of nonbiodegradable plastic materials) and the old potting soil they contain. Nurseries are usually more than happy to take the empty containers off your hands and will reuse them for new products.

The diverse backgrounds, skills, and interests of these entrepreneurs and their willingness to share with us created a wealth of information for you in these pages. We hope you'll take advantage of it. The common trait of all of them is their dedication, which led to success. Let's get started making you a successful entrepreneur, too!

Lawn
Care

Before delving into the intricacies involved in establishing a business, a little background about the businesses of lawn care and landscaping is in order. Although both types of businesses share many characteristics, there are enough differences between them (particularly in terms of the types of services

Soil Testing

offered) that we've chosen to discuss them separately. This chapter focuses solely on lawn care.

If you've been mowing lawns all your life, you already know the basic technique. But did you know that even though a carefully sculpted lawn appears to be beautiful and healthy after being mowed, the mowing process itself is actually bad for all those little green plants? That's because when you mow, you're essentially scalping each tender blade, a process that removes a part of the plant that's used for photosynthesis. You probably remember from high school botany that plants turn sunshine and soil nutrients into their sustenance of sugar, starch, and cellulose. That's why it's not a good idea to crop grass too short during the regular mowing season—you could severely damage those food-making machines. It's also why the experts recommend that you mow often (at least once a week) and remove no more than one-third of the blades each time.

Historical Perspective

Luckily for our lawns, today's mowing technology is much more sophisticated and less damaging compared to the clipping techniques of yesteryear. Before about 1830, people used scythes, those wicked curved blades that are swung in a wide arc and take out anything in their path. As you can imagine, it was pretty hard to get an even trim that way. Back then most yards consisted largely of packed dirt, possibly dotted with flower gardens. Only the wealthy were able to afford bladed ground covers like grass, since they were able to employ a groundskeeper to manicure it. Otherwise, people relied on sheep or cattle to keep their properties shorn. Presidents George Washington and Thomas Jefferson, both of whom were wealthy, kept livestock just for this purpose. Woodrow Wilson also favored the practice, turning his sheep loose to munch the White House lawn in his term from 1913 to 1921.

The first reel lawn mower was invented in 1830, when Edwin Budding, an English textile engineer, realized that a rotary device he had invented for shearing the nap on fabrics might work on grass. It was a timely debut. In the mid-19th century, the American public's perception of the value of green spaces changed when Frederick Law

aha!

Soil testing is useful for lawns that require special treatment, since it measures nutrients in the soil, acidity, and organic matter composition. You can find a qualified soil testing lab online in a Google or www.yellowpages.com search. The test results will help you determine the best way to fertilize, correct acidity, and otherwise care for the lawn.

Olmsted designed new public parks in Boston and New York. People were suddenly drawn to these open green spaces for recreational purposes, and of course this spurred their interest in having lawns of their own. Olmsted nurtured that idea when he laid out the first suburban development in Riverside, Illinois, in 1868. Among his recommendations for what might be considered the country's first subdivision was that the detached homes be set at least 30 feet from the sidewalk—establishing areas that were prime spots for the planting of grass.

The first rotary lawn sprinkler was patented by J. Lessler of Buffalo, New York, in 1871. Coupled with another innovation—the rubber hose—it was possible for the first time to keep lawns watered even in times of drought. Even so, it wasn't easy to maintain a lawn. Early lawn mowers were made of cast iron and could double as cardio workout machines. It wasn't until the 1890s that mowers were motorized; prior to that time, the iron beasts were horse-drawn.

The debut of the first gasoline-powered mowers in the early 1900s changed the process of mowing forever. Also instrumental in creating further interest in turfgrass lawns was the establishment of the first golf course in the United States, Saint Andrews in Ardsley, New York, in 1888. Suddenly golfers themselves became very interested in the quality of the grass they played on, and the U.S. Golf Association funded a number of research studies on grass quality and hybridization. Ultimately, it was studies like these, as well as an influx of imported grasses, improvements in lawn mower design, and the introduction of fertilizer and other lawn chemicals, that made Americans embrace the idea of having their own green piece of earth.

Comparatively speaking, today's lawn mowers (the human kind) have it pretty easy. Now you can just stroll along and let the mower do the hard work, or climb into the driver's seat and put the pedal to the metal. Of course, all this power will cost you (we'll get to that in Chapter 7), but it also means you can do a lot more mowing in a much shorter time. (Translation: You can make more money in less time.)

Business Basics

As you know, lawn maintenance is a seasonal business, with downtime during the winter in about two-thirds of the country. Depending on your area and climate, the

⚠ warning

Anytime you work with gasoline-powered equipment, there's the possibility of sparking a fire, especially in brush country or areas experiencing a drought. Carry a fire extinguisher rated for multiple uses, and make sure your mowers have spark arrestors.

prime growing months run from about April to early October. You'll need to market your services aggressively in the spring so you'll have enough clients to carry you through the summer. In the fall you should be winterizing lawns, raking leaves, and collecting past-due accounts. Still have energy left to spare? During the winter, you can offer services like snow plowing. If you decide to take a well-deserved break instead, you'll have to make sure in advance that you've budgeted wisely throughout the year and have sufficient funds to carry you through those income-free months. (We'll discuss finances in Chapter 13.)

The typical startup lawn care business services 20 to 30 residential clients a week and offers up to three types of services: mowing, fertilizing, and either natural pesticide or chemical application. For the purpose of the lawn care part of this book, we'll focus on mowing and fertilizing, since chemical applications (herbicides, pesticides, and fungicides) are a whole industry unto themselves. With all the information available to us now about the negative effects of unnecessary chemicals in our water, land, and air and their effects on our children and pets, we hope you will choose the most researched, progressive, and safe methods available when developing both the pest control and fertilizing sections of your business. Chemical application is a closely regulated industry that requires practitioners to earn certifications that permit them to handle these hazardous compounds.

Most lawn care service owners prefer to start out with basic mowing and add other services as they become more experienced and acquire more equipment.

> **tip**
>
> Sizing up the competition is an important part of the due diligence you need to do before you launch your business. Check the Yellow Pages (www.yellowpages.com) or Yelp (www.yelp.com), or join Angie's List (www.angieslist.com) to see who's offering which services and whether they offer discounts to seniors or add-on services you haven't thought of.

Grass Attack

Basic lawn maintenance consists of mowing, edging, and trimming. Often, bush and hedge trimming is offered as an extra service, but it's more time consuming and requires more manual dexterity than mowing. Lawn businesses sometimes send out two people to a job site so one person can do the mowing while the other edges and trims the areas the mower can't reach. But if you're a one-person band, you'll just have to allot extra time on each site to complete both jobs. Fortunately, not all lawns have to be edged every time you mow. Sometimes only minor touch-ups are necessary, which you can do using a hand edger.

It's crucial to the survival of your business to keep all your equipment in peak working condition. That means cleaning the mower blades at the end of each day and regularly using a grinding wheel to keep them sharp. You should also use a balancing weight to prolong engine life and to help prevent white finger, a form of Raynaud's disease caused by exposure to constant vibration from equipment like lawn mowers. Clean oil and air filters regularly to keep engine wear to a minimum and improve performance. The oil should also be changed often—as often as once a week, since the high heat of the mower causes lubricants to break down fast.

It goes without saying that you should take every precaution possible to protect yourself while working. Always wear safety goggles and ear protection, and always remember to let your mower cool down completely before you gas it up. Because the cutting blade can rotate at up to 200 miles per hour, never put your hand into the discharge chute or turn the mower over while the blade is spinning. In addition to the obvious injuries it can inflict, that razor-sharp blade can catapult projectiles like rocks, metal, or even compacted grass that can do a body some serious damage.

Spreading the Wealth

If you choose to include fertilizing in your business mix, you'll need a drop spreader. Be sure you practice with it before attacking a customer's lawn, since you can easily burn or unevenly treat the grass, resulting in an unsightly mosaic of sickly green and yellow patches (and the loss of a customer, no doubt). Another option is a broadcast spreader, which

▶ Through the Looking Grass

According to American Lawns (www.American-lawns.com), ". . . Very few turf-type grasses currently growing in America are native to our land. Most turfgrasses were brought to this country and then adapted through selective breeding and cross-breeding to provide us with the grasses that we are most familiar with today." While there are a multitude of grass varieties, American Lawns says there are basically two types:

1. *Cool season*: Kentucky bluegrass, rough bluegrass, red fescue, annual ryegrass, bentgrass, and perennial ryegrass

2. *Warm season*: Bahiagrass, bermudagrass, buffalograss, carpetgrass, centipede, St. Augustine grass, and zoysia grass. There are also transition zone grasses that fall in between the cool and warm regions.

will disperse the fertilizer over a wider area (thus saving you time) but may provide less consistent coverage. No matter which type you use, remember to clean out your spreader well at the end of the day because fertilizers are very corrosive and can damage the hopper.

Guesstimating Your Worth

Another important part of the job is providing estimates to prospective clients. Unfortunately, this is an inexact science, at best. Most of the owners we spoke with "guesstimate" how much time it will take them to mow a homeowner's property, then multiply that by a price per hour. The problem with this method is that land features like slopes and ornamental landscaping can affect the time. For example, let's say it will take you 70 minutes to mow a 10,000-square-foot property using a 22-inch mower. But toss in a backyard that's landscaped with driftwood and rocks and has a raised vegetable garden, and your estimate is no longer quite as accurate.

Experts recommend pricing based on lawn size. It's less arbitrary to set up a pricing structure this way, plus you'll seem more professional to your prospects if you have an established, formal price structure. You can compensate for unusual land features by building an extra amount—say, 10 percent—into your price.

One thing you never want to do, says one California business owner, is to "blind bid," or do an estimate without visiting the property personally. "If you blind bid, then you're a fool and should get out of this business," he says bluntly. "I once bid on a property from hell that hadn't been maintained for two years, and if I hadn't gone over to see it first, I would have lost my shorts."

Bidding in person has another advantage: You can pitch additional services at the same time. For instance, if you're doing a mowing estimate, you might suggest fertilizing, aeration, power mowing, and other add-ons. For a sample estimate form, see Figure 2–1 on page 17.

Establishing Prices

Before you can make an estimate, you have to know how much to charge per square foot. Since the lawn care industry is so competitive, it's important not to overprice your services. The professional organizations and publications that serve the lawn care industry may be able to help, because many of them conduct annual member

aha!

If you're still not sure how much to charge, add up your family's living expenses for the year. Then add in your business expenses. Divide that figure by 2080, which is the average number of working hours per year. The result is the minimum hourly rate you need just to make ends meet.

Estimate for Lawn Services

Date _____

Prepared for:

NAME _____

ADDRESS _____

PHONE _____

Area to be mowed/treated:

_____ Front lawn   _____ square feet

_____ Back lawn   _____ square feet

_____ Full lawn   _____ square feet

Price for weekly mowing service $_____

Price for fertilizer application $ _____ per treatment

Schedule: Every six weeks from March through September

We also offer aeration, power raking, and reseeding at an additional charge. We would be pleased to quote you a price on these services at your request.

Thank you for the opportunity to provide you with this estimate. We'll call you in the next few days to see whether we can be of service. And remember—your satisfaction is always fully guaranteed with Mowing Masters.

Sincerely,

Dan Williams

Dan Williams, Owner

25771 Regal Drive • Kissimmee, Florida 34741 • (555) 555-5555 • mowmasters.com

FIGURE 2–1: **Estimate for Lawn Services**

Feel free to use this example as a template to build your own lawn service estimate form.

studies. You may find *Lawn & Landscape* magazine's State of the Industry Report particularly enlightening, which appears annually in its October issue. You can also figure out how much the market will bear by calculating the size of your own lot and calling a few of the lawn care companies in your area for an estimate. (Typically, owners of lawn care services calculate their prices based on the total square footage of the lot. They can usually estimate roughly how much of a lot is landscaping.) Then recruit a few family members and friends to call for quotes on their lawns, too, so you can get a feel for prices on lots of different sizes. This will help you determine the acceptable price range in your community, and then it's easy to figure out where to price your services. This method works especially well if you're doing business in a community with uniformly platted subdivisions or other similarly sized lots.

fun fact

A 2001 study from the Human-Environment Research Laboratory at the University of Illinois found a striking link between the levels of greenery on residential properties and crime levels. Police crime reports revealed the lowest crime rates on properties with the most vegetation in this study of 98 properties with varying levels of vegetation.

Pricing your services somewhere in the middle or toward the top of the range is a good rule of thumb. You neither want to be the most expensive service in town, nor the cheapest. Demonstrating your professionalism, quality service, and reliability will set you apart from the competition and justify a higher price than the cheapest kid on the block.

Here's another easy way to calculate your fee: Ask the same friends and family members who helped you out by calling your competitors how long it takes them to mow their own lawns. That will give you an idea of the time necessary to mow lots of various sizes. Then use this formula:

Estimated cost of labor + $25 per hour = Your rate per cut

You can play with the $25-per-hour cost, but what it should reflect is your overhead costs (such as phone, office supplies, advertising, equipment, vehicles, etc.) and supplies (like gasoline and trash bags for yard waste removal).

Applying this formula, here's how you would estimate the cost on a 10,000-square-foot lot that takes 55 minutes to mow:

$12	+	$25	=	$37
Estimated labor cost (1 hour @ $12/hour)		Cost factor		Suggested rate

For the sake of simplicity we rounded our labor cost to $12. The current median hourly rate for landscaping and groundskeeping workers is $12.03, according to the U.S. Department of Labor Statistics wage estimates for May 2014. Round your figures up or down according to what you think your market will bear.

Here's another way to calculate your cost factor, based on the amount of money you want to make. Let's say you want to make $30,000 your first year in business. You will be doing business in the Midwest, where you can expect to have about four months of mowing downtime (e.g., November through February). So:

$$\$30,000 \div 32 \text{ weeks} = \$937.50 \text{ per week}$$
$$(\text{eight months})$$
$$(\text{rounded to } \$940)$$
$$\$940 \div 48 = \$19.58/\text{hour}$$
$$(8 \text{ hours a day}$$
$$\text{x } 6 \text{ days/week})$$

Add a 20 percent profit margin   ($3.92)   = $23.50/hour

As you can see, that comes pretty close to the $25 cost factor we mentioned earlier.

Armed with all this information, you'll want to create a pricing schedule sheet that you can refer to when you're asked for a quote. Figure 2–2 on page 20 is a sample of one.

When you actually are asked for a quote, ask the homeowner for the dimensions of his or her lot as a starting point. If the prospect doesn't know, you can use a measuring wheel, available at any home improvement store, to measure both the front yard and backyard of the property. If the land isn't a perfect rectangle (which is often the case), you can make some rough adjustments for the irregular shape. Don't forget to carry a supply of estimate forms and a measuring wheel in your truck at all times. You never know when you might have an opportunity to bid on a new job.

Owners interviewed for this book base their estimates on a visual inspection of the property, and some measured the mowing area as described above. Some charged a flat rate and some charged per hour. How do you know that your prices are in line? Florida landscaper Mike Rosenbleeth says that if 75 percent of the people to whom you give estimates hire you, then your price is about right. Colorado landscaper Kelly Giard charges his clients a monthly rate that never changes, even though the work does. It's kind of like an insurance policy to guarantee the yard will be maintained to a certain caliber that they can budget for. Kelly says they like having a stable rate that they can budget for.

So far, we've been talking only about residential lots. You can apply the same formula to commercial properties. It bears mentioning that it can be harder to land commercial accounts, especially when you're new in the business and haven't built a reputation yet. But

Pricing Schedule

Square Feet	Mowing	Fertilizing	Square Feet	Mowing	Fertilizing
1,000	$29	$18	12,000	$50	$31
1,500	30	18	12,500	50	32
2,000	31	19	13,000	51	33
2,500	32	19	13,500	52	34
3,000	33	20	14,000	53	35
3,500	34	20	14,500	54	36
4,000	35	21	15,000	54	37
4,500	36	21	15,500	55	38
5,000	37	22	16,000	56	39
5,500	38	22	16,500	56	40
6,000	39	23	17,000	57	41
6,500	40	23	17,500	58	42
7,000	41	24	18,000	59	43
7,500	42	24	18,500	60	44
8,000	43	25	19,000	60	45
8,500	44	25	19,500	61	46
9,000	45	26	20,000	62	47
9,500	46	26	20,500	62	48
10,000	46	27	21,000	63	49
10,500	47	28	21,500	64	50
11,000	48	29	22,000	64	51
11,500	49	30			

FIGURE 2–2: **Pricing Schedule Sheet**

it never hurts to try bidding on commercial work, which can be done for everything from golf courses to office and condominium complexes, business parks, and municipal parks.

Ken Walkowski of Armada, Michigan, who retired from his part-time lawn care business, had a single commercial account as the centerpiece of his business—and what a lucrative account it was. He mowed and trimmed the local cemetery, a job that took him four to five days a week twice a month. He also poured cement for headstone foundations (the little platforms the headstones sit on so they don't heave or shift) and serviced 13 residential clients.

"The cemetery job paid well, so I didn't need a lot of customers," says Walkowski, who previously worked for General Motors. "I always landed new business through referrals, and over the years, my customers became more like friends."

Landing a commercial account such as Walkowski's can be challenging, but not impossible. First, call the company you're interested in working for and ask to be put on its bid list. Then you'll be notified when work comes up for bid. You also can take a more proactive approach and send a sales solicitation letter directly to the company and hope for the best. (You'll find a sample letter in Figure 10–4, page 147.) Of course, you'll need property measurements to determine a rate before you send the letter.

The rates charged by the lawn service owners interviewed for this book varied widely, but most charged by the week.

Start Your Engine

The actual lawn care you do will be the single most important part of your regular business day during the summer. But you will also have to attend to numerous other details to keep your business running smoothly and pave the way for additional business later.

To begin with, part of your time will be spent on the phone scheduling jobs, marketing, ordering supplies, and talking to salespeople. Some green professionals believe the time you spend building up your customer base in the first two years should be equal to that of actual lawn care so that you have the option of being selective about the kind of clients you want. Whether or not you decide to put a big part of your energy into marketing in the beginning, you need to stay organized. You can either do this with software or organizational notebooks, although with the inexpensive cost of laptop and tablet computers there is really no reason not to do this electronically. We suggest keeping separate categories such as: current, new, and potential clients (with related logistics and proximity); marketing and social networking channels; new service ideas; research on the top green professionals; expenses and income.

It's important to record details, even if you only have a few clients when you first start out, because creating good habits in the beginning will pay off later by helping you keep your facts straight. Organizational software packages like Real Green do much of this for you, which we'll talk more about in Chapter 7.

Another good reason to map out the details is that you should service all clients located in roughly the same area on the same day—gas prices went on a steady decline for a while but no one thinks that will last forever. Recording types, sizes, and locations will help you cluster mowing jobs and keep you from wasting valuable time crisscrossing your market area (Google Maps provides good directions that can save you a lot of driving). A monthly planner that you keep by your office phone is all you need. Microsoft Office also has a monthly calendar template included with Word that you can use if you prefer to note your appointments electronically, or there are myriad ways (such as an app from Google) to keep electronic calendars that are synchronized with all your electronic devices.

You may decide you want to use a lawn maintenance contract so that your obligations to your customers are spelled out. Turn to Figure 2–3 on page 26 for a sample residential lawn maintenance contract.

Make sure you budget time for marketing and advertising. The part of your advertising that addresses summer services should be done in the spring, right before the start of the regular mowing season. Your winter services, like snow removal, should be marketed in late fall, preferably with a magnetic business card, so that when the snow comes down, there you are, right on the fridge. Occasionally, you'll hear about an advertising opportunity too good to miss, like buying an ad in a recital program for a dance school in an affluent area, or sponsoring a Little League team. You'd then have to spend time creating a new advertising piece. (We'll talk about advertising strategies in Chapter 10.)

If you decide to embark on an adventure and hire some employees, you'll have yet another task to add to your daily agenda: personnel management. In addition to coordinating their schedules, you'll need to train them after you've spent time hunting for them in the first place.

Finally, general office administration will take up a chunk of your time. This will include returning phone calls, handling the finances (i.e., accounts payable and receivable), giving instructions to employees, rescheduling work hampered by weather, and sending out invoices.

Getting paid for your services should be simple and not take a lot of time. Tension can build if customers don't respond to invoices in a timely fashion, and it can damage

tip

Call up 20 of the top-rated green industry professionals across the United States (but not in your state). You can find them by searching on Yelp and the Better Business Bureau site (www.bbb.org). Tell them you are starting a similar business in another state and ask if they'd be willing to give you a 15-minute informational interview on their business practices for mentorship purposes. Write down what you like and dislike about each company to help shape your vision.

your relationship with them. You wind up giving second and third notices, and this can create unnecessary friction between you and your customer. Sometimes they're running behind with all of their bills, or having tough financial times, or simply just too busy to send it in. None of these personal problems that customers have should become your problem, but life isn't that simple, is it?

Kelly Giard uses a system for Clean Air Lawn Care that seems to eliminate a lot of these issues. He requires his clients to submit a credit card number, even if they're paying by check. Most of his customers are enrolled in an electronic, automatic billing, flat monthly rate program, so there are no invoices or waiting for checks to be written and sent. Their bill is deducted from their bank account on the fifth day of each month for that month. The few people that pay him by check usually pay by the tenth, and if they don't, Kelly doesn't need to interrupt their monthly service agreement, because he can just charge it to their credit card.

If you want to use hard copies to deliver an actual paper invoice, ServiceCEO offers a handy invoicing and tracking system with many customizing features. Take a look at how it can help you here: www.insightdirect.com. You can also keep it very simple in the beginning when you just have a handful of customers by using a preprinted invoice form from your local office supply store that you leave inside the customer's screen door or rubber band it to the knob. It's not necessary to speak to customers at all, and in fact, they will probably appreciate that you didn't interrupt them just to hand over a bill. But don't leave your bill in the mailbox. It's considered private property, and it's illegal to use it for anything other than mail delivered by a USPS carrier. You can keep a book of invoice forms (available at office supply stores) in your truck and handwrite the bill at every stop.

Second, you could generate your invoices at the end of the month and mail them all at once. This will necessitate stuffing envelopes and spending money on postage, but sending a bill through the mail gives the impression that you're a professional who takes the business seriously.

aha!

When you do lawn maintenance, you're the expert on what works best and what should be done to improve the property. So be sure to recommend additional services like fertilizing or aeration, and always inform the homeowner about the presence of pests like moles, or conditions like snow mold. Try to use a humane pest control professional who traps and relocates the critters instead of using poison. You'll look good, improve the property, and make some extra money all at the same time.

Staffing

It's common for people to start lawn care businesses as one-person operations, and with good reason: It keeps the monthly costs manageable. But the day may come, perhaps sooner than you expect, when you have more work than you can handle alone. That's the time to think about adding employees so you don't have to turn down work that could make the company grow.

Sometimes you can simply hire an assistant who can accompany you on jobs and help you get the work done twice as fast. With a big spurt in business, however, you may have to add a second crew. In either case, the decision to hire shouldn't be made lightly because it takes a lot of time, effort, and money to find and train employees. You'll find an extensive discussion of employees in Chapter 8, but for now, it's enough to know that the most common types of employee used by lawn care services are: general maintenance assistants, who do mowing, weed whacking, and other lawn maintenance duties; certified chemical applicators, who apply fertilizer, pesticides, and herbicides; and office assistants, who answer phones, handle accounts payable/receivable, and otherwise keep your office operations in tip-top shape.

Some lawn care service owners prefer to use subcontractors rather than hire employees, especially for jobs like chemical application, which, in most states, requires certification. In essence, contractors work for you and bill you for their time and materials. Then you turn around, mark up the service 15 to 25 percent (standard in this industry), and bill the cost to your customer. This might sound great, but using subcontractors is not without challenges. Refer to Chapter 8 for more information about the employer-subcontractor relationship and how you can stay on the right side of the IRS when you use such workers.

▶ Pricing Schedule

Homewyse (www.Homewyse.com) allows you to calculate the cost of mowing a lawn by plugging in a zip code and square footage. For example, an East Coast zip code prices out at an average of $47.25 to mow a 500-square-foot lawn with an average cost per square foot of around 9.5 cents.

Take this to the West Coast in an upscale Los Angeles zip code, and your price nearly doubles to 21 cents per square foot.

Weathering the Storm(s)

Even in the sunniest of climes, you are likely to have days when you can't mow or plant or prune—like when the winds reach hurricane speed or you notice your neighbor is building an ark. There's not much you can do when grass and landscaping are wet—except maybe catch up on paperwork, lust over equipment catalogs, and read email. That's why many green industry service providers choose to work a five-day workweek, leaving Saturdays (and Sundays, if necessary) unscheduled just in case the weather wreaks havoc on their work plans. Alternatively, you can work longer hours on a regular maintenance day to catch up—chances are people won't even blink if you're out merrily mowing or trimming as the sun is setting because it means they don't have to.

There's one more weather phenomenon you may actually welcome, at least in the northern tier of the country. Snow plowing can be a very lucrative mainstay or sideline to add to your lawn or landscaping business. It doesn't cost much to launch a snow removal service—basically you need only a snow blade for your mower or truck and some extra advertising efforts. (Food for thought: Michigan landscaper Michael Collins reports that he gets 70 percent of his snow plowing business through his website.) Best of all, offering such a service means you'll have a regular income stream even during the slowest part of the year.

Marc Wise and Lindsay Stame of Greenwise Organic Lawncare in Evanston, Illinois, can count on a lot of snow to support their supplemental plowing service during the harsh Midwestern winters, as well as the growing demand for applications of their eco-friendly ice melt product that is safe for pets, plants, and the water table. They also offer an LED light-hanging service for the holiday season and create seasonal displays for events.

Now that you're in the know about the lawn care industry, read on in Chapter 3 for information about landscaping business opportunities.

Residential Lawn Maintenance Contract

Part I—Lawn Maintenance

A. Mowing, edging, and trimming. Contractor will mow turf areas as needed according to seasonal growth. Mowing shall be done with a reel, rotary, or mulching mower, and mowing height will be according to grass type and variety. Contractor will leave clippings on the lawn as long as no readily visible clumps remain on the grass surface 36 hours after mowing. Otherwise, contractor will distribute large clumps of clippings by mechanical blowing or by collecting and removing them. In the case of fungal disease outbreaks, contractor will collect clippings until the disease is undetectable.

Contractor will edge tree rings and plant beds, and all surfaced areas bordered by grass (i.e., sidewalks, fences, driveways) every other mowing during the growing season. Isolated trees and shrubs growing in lawn areas will require mulched areas around them (minimum two-foot diameter) to avoid bark injury from mowers and filament line trimmers and to reduce root competition from grass. Establishment and maintenance of such mulched areas will be charged to the customer. Contractor will clean all clippings from sidewalks, curbs, and roadways immediately after mowing and/or edging. Contractor will not sweep, blow or otherwise dispose of clippings in sewer drains. The cost of these services is $_____ (weekly, monthly, annually).

B. Fertilization. Contractor will fertilize turf areas as per the maintenance specifications (attached). Fertilizer will be swept off of walks and drives onto lawns or beds. After fertilization, a minimum of 1/4 inch of water will be applied by the client. The cost of these services is $_____ (weekly, monthly, annually).

C. Pest control. The contractor will inspect lawn areas during each visit for indications of pest problems and advise the client of such problems. Upon confirmation of a specific problem requiring treatment, the contractor will apply pesticides as needed and only in affected spots, using the least toxic, most effective pesticide whenever possible. The cost of these services is $_____ (weekly, monthly, annually). The pest control applicator operates under

License #_____, expiration date _____.

Part II—Insurance, Licenses, Permits, and Liability

The contractor will carry liability amounts and workers' compensation coverage required by law on his/her operators and employees and require same of any subcontractors and provide proof of same to the client. The contractor is also responsible for obtaining any licenses and/or permits required by law for activities on client's property.

FIGURE 2–3: **Residential Lawn Maintenance Contract**

Although you may decide to use a briefer and less formal lawn contract, here are some of the items you may wish to include.

Residential Lawn Maintenance Contract

Situations that the contractor may deem are his/her responsibility:

1. Any damage due to operation of his equipment in performing the contract.
2. Damage to plant material due to improper horticultural practices.
3. Injury to nontarget organisms due to application of pesticides.

Situations that the Contractor may deem are not his/her responsibility:

1. Death or decline of plant materials due to improper selection, placement, planting, or maintenance done before the time of this contract.
2. Flooding, storm, wind, fire, or cold damages.
3. Disease or damage to lawns or landscape plants caused by excessive irrigation or lack of water due to inoperative irrigation components provided he/she reported these to client, or irrigation restrictions imposed by civil authorities.

Part III—Property Description and Terms

1. Contract applies to the property at:

   _____

   _____

2. The term of this contract is

   _____ One year beginning (date) _____

   _____ March-November, 20_____

   _____ Until written cancellation is received

   _____ Other (specify) _____

Customer signature: _____   Date _____

Contractor signature: _____   Date _____

FIGURE 2–3: **Residential Lawn Maintenance Contract,** continued

Landscaping

Ah, wilderness! Nature calls to those who listen to its irresistible siren's song, coaxing us to slow down and explore it, enjoy its sights, sounds, and scents, and immerse ourselves in its peacefulness. That is, of course, unless you are an aspiring landscaper, in which case you probably yearn to fire up your gas- or electric-powered trimmers and tame those wayward plants and trees around you into pristine perfection.

Landscapers come in all shapes, sizes, and backgrounds, but they all share one thing in common: a genuine love of the outdoors and growing things. It's what drives them to spend most of every day on the job covered in dirt. It induces them to learn the Latin names of plants, shrubs, and trees—on purpose. It also makes them gleefully haul around 45-gallon containers (and the redwoods sprouting from them) like child's play rather than actual work. Sound like fun? Then you've come to the right place. This chapter explores the various ways you can enter this interesting and fulfilling profession, and provides an overview of the day-to-day activities involved in running your own landscaping empire.

Historical Perspective

The profession of landscaping may be fairly new, historically speaking, but landscaping your environment to beautify it, as well as to do more utilitarian things like halt erosion and create wind barriers, probably has been around as long as humankind itself. Some historians believe that the desire to place your imprint on the environment stems from ancient humans' belief in mysticism and rituals. Certainly there are many examples of this mysticism still in existence today: the cave paintings of Lascaux, France, which date back to the Ice Age in the Upper Paleolithic Age; the towering megaliths of Stonehenge on the Salisbury Plain in southern England (2,750 to 1,500 B.C.), which are considered the greatest example ever of landscaping with stone; and the mysterious pyramids of Egypt and Mexico. These structures illustrate that humans have always felt the need to tailor their surroundings to their own aesthetic preferences.

The earliest known garden plans date back to Egypt, circa 1400 B.C. But perhaps the most famous example of early landscaping is the Hanging Gardens of Babylon, which are known as one of the Seven Wonders of the Ancient World. According to written accounts by ancient Greeks like Strabo and Philo of Byzantium, the gardens were built near the River Euphrates by Nebuchadnezzar II (who ruled from 604 to 562 B.C.) and "consist[ed] of

aha!

Consider the architectural style you are designing green for and match accordingly. Match bold architecture with sturdy, bold plants and refined and understated architecture with softer, more delicate colors, textures, and arrangements. See www.finegardening.com for inspiration and matching tips.

arched vaults which are located on checkered cubelike foundations . . . The ascent of the uppermost terrace-roofs is made by a stairway . . ."

That might sound like Greek to us now, but it made perfect sense to other civilizations, which emulated that technique of turning steep slopes into flat, usable garden space. For instance, terraces have festooned Himalayan mountainsides in Nepal for thousands of years, while more recently the Incans built elaborate terraces in the mountains of Peru so they could grow potatoes and grain. Of course, the French have cultivated grapes on such terraced slopes.

aha!

Houses painted in unusual colors (anything other than neutrals like beige, gray, or white) look best with plantings in dark green and white. But you can accent the home by repeating the house color in nearby plantings.

As might be expected, early American landscaping mirrored that of Europe—England in particular—since the early colonial settlers brought with them visions in their heads of the elaborate gardens they left behind. For nearly 300 years—until the 18th century—the Italian formal garden style had influenced European landscaping, although by the 1730s, English gardens (or jardins anglais) also were inspired by the geometric designs of French gardens and the topiaries used by the Dutch.

American gardens emulated this pattern, which by then also featured grass lawns and gravel walkways. In the 1830s (not coincidentally, when the first lawn mower was invented), landscaped cemeteries and public parks began to sprout around the country, no doubt because only the very wealthy could afford to set aside land for purely ornamental purposes. In fact, in the 1834 edition of *The Encyclopedia of Gardening*, J.C. Loudon wrote, "Landscape gardening is practiced in the United States on a comparatively limited scale . . . the only splendid example of park and hot house gardening that . . . will ever be found are such that will be formed by towns, villages, or other communities."

Loudon was wrong, of course. During the Victorian period (1850 to 1900), American gardeners had access to a wide variety of plants, thanks to the explorations of Lewis and Clark, and took to gardening enthusiastically. From there it was just a matter of time before decorative touches like statuary, fountains, pergolas (a type of Italian-influenced outdoor structure often used to cover a passageway), and early lawns that were no more than grass panels planted next to walkways found their way into modern garden landscapes. Industry innovations like the lawn sprinkler, which was patented in 1871, also hastened the establishment of residential gardens, as did the debut of the first American golf course. St. Andrews in Ardsley, New York, was developed in a cow pasture in 1888, and showed middle-class Americans what large-scale landscaping design was all about.

It wasn't until the mid-20th century that lawns truly became mainstream. Prior to that time, they were difficult to cultivate, partly because most grasses are not native to the North American continent. By the '50s, the use of imported grasses, hybrids, irrigation, and fertilizers, as well as improvements in lawn mower design, made it possible for virtually every homeowner to have the lawn and landscape of his or her dreams.

Types of Landscaping Businesses

There are numerous ways you can forge a business in either residential or commercial landscaping—or both. Some of the fields require more than just a love of gardening to succeed—they also require experience and formal education (which we'll discuss in Chapter 9). The major career paths for landscapers include:

▶ *Gardener/groundskeeper.* This type of green industry professional is usually in charge of keeping up appearances—he or she may care for plants and other greenery, and may perform that work in a garden, greenhouse, or work shed. What sets gardeners and groundskeepers apart from other landscape professionals is that they normally don't do any design work; rather, they tend existing landscapes, although they may render other services like applying pesticides and herbicides, mowing lawns, doing spring and fall cleanups, composting, etc. They need a good working knowledge of horticulture and plant varieties.

▶ *Interiorscaper* (aka interior landscaper). You can build an entire business caring for plants in office buildings, shopping malls, and other public places. Interior landscapers are usually contractors who provide general maintenance and care, as well as give advice about the types of plants and planters that will best complement a building's interior design. Interiorscapers often give advice about plant selection, supervise and/or set up or tear down holiday decorations, and offer other services that are loosely related to interior design. While you don't need a design background to be successful, it helps if you have an eye for color, shape, texture, and form and can translate that into green focal points that will complement beautifully arranged interiors.

▶ *Landscaper.* In the most general sense, this is the type of person who installs and maintains plants, flowers, trees, sod, and other natural materials like rocks and mulch. Lawn care often is part of the landscape maintenance professional's menu of services, plus he or she may also offer basic design services (a good eye and an equally good design software package make it possible). Finally, landscapers may offer add-on services, such as sprinkler installation or hardscape construction, to stay busy. We'll discuss the numerous ways you can pump up your business a little later. Most states require landscapers to be licensed. Check with your state's department of licensing, labor, or contracting board to find out the requirements.

▶ *Landscape architect/designer.* Planning verdant spaces is the job of the landscape architect (aka landscape designer). Landscape architects often work side by side with building architects, surveyors, and engineers to design and plan projects like new subdivisions, public parks, college campuses, shopping centers, golf courses, and industrial parks, and then produce detailed drawings to pull the projects together. They may specialize in a certain type of project, such as waterfront development, site construction, or environmental remediation (e.g., preserving wetlands). Landscape architects also play an important role in historic landscape preservation and restoration.

fun fact

Electric mowers continue to improve. TopTenReviews (www. toptenreviews.com) listed the 2016 best as the Kobalt 40-volt cordless mower with a list price of $349 that is described as a great mower for mid- to large-size lawns and comes with a convenient extra battery. Next in line is the EGO LM 2001, which retails at a hefty $499 but boasts a 30-minute battery charge time.

This is the most technical of the four and a bachelor's or master's degree in landscape architecture is usually required to enter the field. If you already hold a degree in another field, you may be able to pursue a three-year master's degree in landscape architecture to get the background you need. According to the American Society of Landscape Architects, 69 colleges and universities offer undergraduate or graduate programs in landscape architecture that are accredited by the Landscape Architecture Accreditation Board. (We will discuss some of these programs in Chapter 9.) Most states require licensing or registration for practitioners in the field, which means you will be required to take and pass a proficiency exam, and renew and pay for the license every year. Licensed landscape architects charge the highest fees, which is why in 2015 the median pay of landscape architects was $63,810 per year, according to *Occupational Outlook Handbook.*

There are many other plant-related businesses that might be of interest to landscapers, including silviculturist (someone who specializes in the care of trees, especially relating to forests), horticulturist (a person who investigates better ways to grow, harvest, and store fruits, vegetables, and ornamental plants), and turf specialist (someone who cares for turf and sod). You can find an extensive list of horticulture and landscape design-related businesses on the Vocational Information Guide website at www.khake.com. But for the purposes of this book, we will assume you are interested in a business in one of the four professions discussed above.

By the way, just because you have decided on a selected slate of services, there's no reason you can't break the rules a little if it keeps the business flowing in. For instance, Michael Collins, the Livonia, Michigan, landscaping business co-owner, actually started doing more lawn maintenance than landscaping, and plans to continue in that vein—at least for the short term. The reason? There are many new subdivisions with upscale homes within a ten-mile radius of his business, so it makes sense to cultivate that business first because it could open the door to landscaping jobs later.

Scope of Services

One of the first things you should do in the early stages of establishing a new landscaping business is determine exactly which services you'd like to perform. You probably already have a pretty good idea of what a landscaper does, especially if you've been mowing lawns since you were a kid or you're now lovingly looking after your own property. To help you decide which services might be of interest to you, let's take a look at the full range of activities a landscaper might take on.

Gardening/Maintenance

Among the basic landscaping services are:

- ▶ *Mowing*: followed by cleaning up lawn debris with a blower
- ▶ *Edging*: to give lawns a straight edge and a finished look
- ▶ *Fertilizing*: to make those blades grow
- ▶ *Controlling pests*: to eliminate critters that feed on or otherwise damage turf
- ▶ *Weeding and controlling weeds*: not much fun, but a necessary job
- ▶ *Watering*: either manually or by using an automatic sprinkler system
- ▶ *Core aerating*: loosening or puncturing the soil to increase the ability of water and air to penetrate, which improves plant growth

tip

Before leaving a worksite, take a quick look around to make sure every task has been completed and no tools have been left behind. It's also helpful to note your start and finish times, since this information can come in handy the next time you're trying to estimate how long a similar job will take.

▶ Paying the Pump

Paying for gasoline and oil changes, vehicle maintenance and tolls in the course of doing business is a way of life for landscapers. But when gasoline costs are growing faster than a weed or a municipality dramatically hikes its toll charges, it can have a negative impact on landscapers. That's why it's not unusual in this industry to charge a mileage-based fuel surcharge to help offset those costs, particularly if you have a very large service area.

To figure out an equitable charge, look to the IRS for direction. For 2016, the IRS has set the mileage rate at a 54-cents-per-mile deduction for business-related travel. Suppose you're located in the center of a service area that's about 20 miles in diameter. Your fuel surcharge to go to the furthest point in your market area from your home base would be $5.40 (10 miles x 54 cents). Of course, there could be days when you'll be finishing up a reflecting pond job in the morning on one side of town and then driving 20 miles back across town to another job site ($5.40 x 2 = $10.80).

Let's face it—you could end up spending all your time calculating surcharges if you assess them on a job-by-job basis. It makes better business sense to come up with a standard charge—say, around $8.50 in this case—and use it for every customer, no matter where the job site is. Just be aware that fuel surcharges can cause hard feelings, especially since your clients will be feeling the pinch of higher gas prices, too. It may be wiser to fold that charge into your quote without calling attention to it as an itemized charge.

- ▶ *Composting*: turning yard and food waste into organic matter
- ▶ *Reseeding*: to repair barren spots or areas that have been exposed to disease
- ▶ *Topdressing*: adding topsoil on top of a plant to improve the soil beneath
- ▶ *Repairing sprinkler heads*: to keep that water coming for a thirsty lawn
- ▶ *Setting automatic sprinkler timers*: to help those who are keypad-challenged
- ▶ *Trimming and pruning*: to keep both plants and trees neat and tidy
- ▶ *Doing general seasonal cleanups*: in the spring to prepare the ground for new growth, and/or in the fall to remove dead organic material like leaves. Consider tacking on a pet waste pickup service to your offerings. Weekly rates listed by Pet Scoop in Colorado (www.petscoop.com) are $9.90 per dog for an average-sized yard once per week. Twice-per-week cleanups are less per cleanup. Pet Scoop guarantees owner satisfaction or offers a "re-doo."
- ▶ *Removing snow*: a winter-season revenue generator, to be sure

Installation

If you like working with soil and helping things grow, you might consider offering the following installation services, either as a mainstay of or extra service for your business:

▶ Lawn, plant, and tree installation

▶ Sod installation

▶ Lawn seeding

▶ Hydroseeding: applying a watery slurry of seed, fertilizer, soil binder, and/or mulch, which sprouts and fills in rapidly

▶ Tree transplanting, guying, and staking

▶ Power raking to remove thatch, the layer of dead plant material that piles up between the soil and the grass, or moss, which can choke off the grass if it gets out of control

▶ Underground drainage system installation, including curtain drains, French drains, catch basins, etc., to solve problems with water that flows away too quickly or pools, leaving a lawn or garden waterlogged

▶ Automatic sprinkler system and other irrigation device installation, including automatic valve and timer systems

▶ Grading to prepare soil for plant installation

▶ Mailbox installation in demand in new subdivisions

▶ Seasonal turn-on and shut-down of in-ground sprinkler systems

▶ General lawn renovation: usually offered as a package of services that may include fertilizing, power raking, topdressing, rolling, and other services

▶ General landscape renovation to fill in, restore, or otherwise improve existing landscaping

Special Construction

The following types of hardscaping projects can be real moneymakers, even though each type of job may require special equipment that you must purchase or rent. Depending on your level of training, expertise, and willingness, you could offer to build or install:

▶ *Fences and walls.* Erected to protect landscaping from the elements, increase privacy, or establish property boundaries; may be freestanding or retaining, and may be constructed of wood (including the ever-popular railroad tie), natural stone, precast stone, or green materials, including ornamental shrubbery like pines, firs, etc. Hedges are considered outdoor walls.

► *Living walls, biowalls, and vertical gardens.* Stand out from the crowd by offering this unique and artistic service, which will still require grooming maintenance from you as you grow a reputation as the only service provider in your area to offer them. These vertical structures home thriving plants and have inner structures designed for easy trickle-down watering. See these innovators for examples, construction ideas, and material sources: www.livingwallart.com, www.fosterplants.com, and www.verticalgardenpatrickblanc.com.

► *Rock gardens.* To add dimension to landscaping while giving plants a place to thrive

► *Borders.* Typically installed to create a line of demarcation between ornamental planting beds and lawns; may be made of wood, plastic, metal, brick, or decorative stone

► *Paths, walks, stepping stones, and driveways.* Used to unite areas or separate one area from another (e.g., the lawn from the garden), or to provide access to the house, yard, and other areas, including landscaped areas that require maintenance. Brick pavers and other irregularly shaped materials like gravel, flagstones, and even broken concrete are often used.

► *Steps.* Often used to move between landscaping on several levels or link flat areas like lawns or terraces; often serve as a unique garden feature on their own merit.

► *Decks and patios.* These help to establish usable outdoor space and "living rooms" for entertaining. Patios are usually constructed at ground level of stone or concrete, while decks are raised platforms of pressure-treated or rot-resistant wood that may or may not be attached to the home.

► *Shade/storage structures.* Whether strictly ornamental (like gazebos and pavilions) or functional (like sheds), these buildings are outdoor rooms that can be constructed at a modest cost.

► *Ornamental structures.* Used to diffuse direct sunlight or to provide support for climbing plants and vines; structures like arbors, pergolas, and trellises are usually constructed over patios, decks, or bare ground to provide a covered walkway or shady area. Ideally, they unite the house style with the landscaping theme. While usually made of wood, these structures also may be constructed of metal poles topped with canvas.

► *Landscaping and exterior lighting.* Includes low-voltage path lighting, downlighting (usually as a security measure), and uplighting (to emphasize distinctive features like the building's façade or landscaping).

► *Solar installations for night gardens.* Collecting energy from the sun, solar products glow in many forms and colors. You can create a night garden by designing with solar implements, such as glowing violets, birds, hanging stars, and gazing globes.

Intersperse that lovely illumination with kinetic sculpture and your cleverly lit landscaping and you've created a midnight wonderland. See www. gardenfun.com, www.sunnysolarlightgarden. com, Walmart, Amazon, and Home Depot to name a few places that carry solar lights and stepping stones.

> **tip**
>
> Need help with estimating? Try one of these books: *Landscape Estimating Methods* (R. S. Means Co.) by Sylvia Hollman Fee, and *Landscape Estimating and Contract Administration* (Delmar CengageLearning) by Stephen Angley, et al.

► *Seasonal staging.* Decorative additions to home exteriors set a "ministage" to create a mood. Autumn calls for playful displays of hay bales, scarecrows, baskets of gourds, and topiaries made of changing leaves. Winter holidays usually entail hanging lights, but if you add some creativity and think of an antique sleigh, mistletoe-wrapped mailbox, and wheelbarrow full of faux sugar plums and pinecones, you've got yourself a staging service. Keep a photographic portfolio on hand and start your sales pitch on this service two months early.

► *Water features.* Often built to complement ornamental plantings or to provide a tranquil oasis. Typical residential water features include Asian-inspired garden pools, water gardens, ponds, and fountains. Waterfalls, reflecting pools, and streams are also popular choices for larger yards.

► *Petscaping.* Design process that takes into consideration the patterns of domestic and wild animals to create harmony for and between the animals and homeowner. Most often petscaping refers to creating dog-friendly yards that are easy to maintain. Dogs wear down a path while "patrolling" the perimeter of their yards, so pebble, stone, or woodchip paths are implemented there to complement the high traffic zone. Astroturf is being used as a way to combat grass burn from companion animal elimination. Mixing children and pets in a yard is much more hygienic when there is a designated potty area away from the play area, which can actually be decorative. Designing for wildlife takes all of this into consideration as well, along with ways to keep them safe and separate from companion animals. Michigan landscaper Tom Barthel's book, *Dogscaping*, has in-depth instruction. *Dog Friendly Gardens, Garden Friendly Dogs*, by Cheryl S. Smith also has creative ideas for this growing trend.

Other hardscaping installations often requested by homeowners are decorative features like flagpoles, sculptures, birdhouses and feeders, benches, and mailboxes.

General Business Operations

While you have many choices when customizing your new landscaping business, there are certain tasks that you'll need to do no matter which services you choose to offer. They include the following.

Estimating Jobs

Whether you're providing a simple service like pruning bushes or you're installing an elaborate three-level deck, people will want to know upfront how much a job will cost. As a result, it's imperative to develop good estimating skills right from the start. The trouble is, estimating is a science, and it's easy to make a misstep that could cost you plenty in terms of time and resources.

There are a number of software packages (like CLIP and LandPro Systems) developed specifically for landscapers that you can use to help you make good estimates. We've also listed the names of a few books in the Appendix that you might find helpful. In the meantime, here is a general overview of how to go about making an educated guess.

Your mission here is to determine what your costs will be and then add in a profit. Your costs will include everything from materials (plants, mulch, topsoil, etc., which you have marked up from your wholesale or retail price) to labor (both your own employees and subcontractors), equipment (yours and any you rent), and your general business overhead (anything you plan to claim as the cost of doing business, such as home office expenses, gasoline, etc.).

Your estimate should outline the exact services you're offering, materials you'll provide, and anything else pertinent to the job. The standard in this industry is to provide an estimate free of charge and is what we recommend. See Figure 3-1, "Materials Estimate," on page 40.

Once you have secured a job, you should put the terms of the agreement in writing. This not only protects you, but it's also a requirement in many states. A written bid is also helpful because if you're ever asked to provide any additional services while you're on the job (something

tip

Even though you'll probably have to squeeze estimating into your workday, it's unacceptable to show up dirty and sweaty. Try to schedule estimates either at the beginning of the day before you get dirty or at the end of the day so you can clean up first. Or keep a clean shirt and hand cleaner in your truck so you can change before knocking on a potential client's door.

Materials Estimate

Date: _____

Homeowner name: _____

Property address: _____

Phone number: _____

Property measurements: _____

Lawn size: _____ Bed size: _____

Quantity	Materials	Unit Price	Line Total
		Subtotal	
		Sales tax	
		TOTAL	

FIGURE 3–1: **Materials Estimate Form**

that happens all the time), you have every right to charge extra because those services are not spelled out in the terms of the original agreement. At the very least, always get your customer's signature on a work order at the start of the job. That will prevent any misunderstandings later and gives you a legal leg to stand on in the event a client defaults on the financial terms of the agreement.

Incidentally, landscaping experts recommend having a standard contract even for maintenance jobs. As with a bid, these contracts also give full details about the extent of the service you're providing.

The only time you really don't need to have a formal contract is when you are providing one-time or basic services, such as sprinkler head repair or seasonal cleanup. In that case, you can simply present a bill when the work is finished. To estimate this type of job, you can use the time and materials basis method, which means you estimate the time, multiply that by your labor rate (actual + profit margin), and add in your materials costs to arrive at a reasonable rate.

warning

There's a difference between estimating and quoting. An estimate is a general idea of how much a job will cost. A quote is the price you agree to charge for the work. Although your customers would prefer a quote, landscaping professionals suggest giving only estimates so you're protected if the job comes in higher than you expected.

Finally, to make an accurate guess on what to charge, be sure to make a site visit. Consider every aspect of the topography when you scope out the area, including grade, type of soil, and structures and other features (decks, rock gardens, etc.).

In addition to garnering new business with estimates, Michael Collins, the Michigan landscaper, has found another way to put his estimates to work. He includes information about his referral service, which awards any current customer with a price cut on the next service for referring new customers, with both his estimates and quotes. He says the practice has netted him new business that he otherwise might have missed out on.

Setting Prices

Of course, before you can give an estimate, you have to come up with a price you can use as a baseline. Landscaping professionals recommend coming up with an hourly rate, both for yourself and your employees. But you won't be sharing that rate with your customers—it's for your eyes only, so you can figure out how much to charge for a job.

There are many ways to determine your rate. First, you can compare your prices to those of your competition. Enlist the help of friends and family to help you contact companies in your target market area that offer services similar to what you plan to offer. If you're doing business in an area that has a lot of subdivisions with similar-size homes and lots, the process will be relatively easy.

Another good way to determine your rate is to figure out how much it would cost you to, say, install sod (materials plus labor), and then divide that amount by the number of hours it would take you to complete the job. Add a profit margin, and you'll have a number you can use.

Finally, you can figure your rate based on how much money you'd like to make in a given year. For example, if your goal is to make $40,000 during your first year in business, you need to earn approximately $3,334 per month ($40,000 divided by 12). If you want to work 35 hours a week, a four-week month would be 140 hours a month. Divide $3,334 by 140 to arrive at a rate of $23.81 per hour. You can mark that cost up (or at least round it up), then add in your profit margin. Naturally, your cost of doing business, which includes materials, tool costs, and office administration costs, would be billed to customers in addition to this hourly rate.

In the end it doesn't matter how you arrive at your rate as long as you make enough money to meet your monthly obligations. When determining your rate, think about how much you need to pay the business bills and cover your personal expenses (including the mortgage, health insurance, and other household bills). When you can pay all the bills and

► Price Shopping

Although it's customary to mark up the products and supplies you purchase for use on the job, you'll want to get them at the best possible prices so you don't have to pass along excessive charges to your customers. For that reason, you should establish a network of suppliers who will give you a discount on the plants and other materials you'll routinely need.

If you're a licensed contractor, you'll be able to purchase materials at wholesale directly from growers and wholesalers. Even if you end up buying retail at a garden center (like when you need just a few plants to fill in an empty space, or an extra roll of edging for a flower bed), you might be able to negotiate a small discount in appreciation of your recurring business (say, 10 to 20 percent).

When it comes to materials for other hardscape projects like irrigation system parts, lighting, or lumber, you'll need to do a little scouting to find businesses in your area that sell to tradespeople. These companies should be willing to offer you a discount because they know you'll be a source of repeat business.

still have some cash left over to funnel back into the business or salt away in a business account, then you've priced your services appropriately.

Scheduling Jobs

In the early days of running your business, it will be easy to figure out where you need to be on any given day. But when the phone starts ringing, you may find yourself scrambling to coordinate jobs, and unless you have a good system for tracking those jobs, you could miss an appointment—and lose a customer. Therefore, you might want to invest in a software package designed especially for landscapers to help you track your business. You'll find information about some of these packages in Chapter 7, and you can find a list of software in the Appendix.

Once you've entered data into these programs, you can print out a schedule for the day that you can carry with you in your vehicle. Always remember to build travel time into your schedule and use an online mapping site like Google Maps to plan your route for the day.

A Day in the Life

While your reason for entering the landscaping field may be to get your hands dirty as you beautify America one home at a time, you'll have a lot of other duties to attend to as the owner of a newly minted small business. Some of the office tasks you'll handle during a typical workday include:

▶ *Office administration.* Besides answering the phone and email, you'll have mail to open and bills to send out and pay. If you decide to accept credit cards, you'll also have to process those credit cards through your merchant account. (You'll find information about merchant accounts in Chapter 13.) Be prepared for it to take a substantial amount of time—as much as two to three hours per day—to do the books. If you're numerically challenged, you might want to hire an accountant. (We'll discuss finding an accountant and other types of business professionals in Chapter 6.)

▶ *Customer service.* Tasks include fielding requests for estimates and scheduling appointments, both for estimates and actual jobs.

▶ *Purchasing.* You'll need to buy supplies for the business, including office supplies, tools needed for the job, and chemicals like fertilizer.

▶ *Personnel management.* Once you find you need employees, you'll have to spend time interviewing candidates, overseeing employees' work, making up work schedules, and refereeing when conflict arises.

Staffing

Speaking of employees, you probably won't be ready to hire anyone right away. But when you have more work than you can personally handle, you may need to take the plunge into boss-ship. Chapter 8 is devoted to a discussion of where to find employees and how to work with them once you bring them aboard. In the meantime, here are the types of employee you may find you need:

▶ General landscaping assistants for mowing, maintenance, and installation assistance.

▶ Licensed chemical applicator for both fertilizing and pesticide/herbicide applications. Most states require licensure or certification for workers who apply pesticides and herbicides.

▶ An estimator for doing site visits, sizing up the work, and generating estimates for customers.

▶ General office staff for handling office administration when you get too busy to do it yourself.

Instead of hiring a whole bunch of people and taking on the big expense that comes along with employees, or if you really don't need permanent staff, you can contract out the services you can't handle yourself to carefully selected subcontractors. For instance, you could subcontract out the building of a deck to an experienced carpenter, engage the services of a landscape architect to handle the design of a whole-yard installation, or pay a licensed chemical applicator to handle all your pesticide/herbicide applications. Your customer doesn't have to know you're using a subcontractor—and in fact, it can be even less transparent to them if you give your subcontractors a T-shirt or baseball cap with your company name on it to wear while on the job.

When you subcontract services, your subcontractors will bill you, and then you should add a markup of 15 to 25 percent to the bill you send to the client. This is not gouging—it's a way to cover the overhead and administrative costs you incur in the course of doing business. Just be sure to screen your subcontractors carefully before hiring them. Anyone who does work for you is a representative of your business, and can help or hurt your reputation depending on the quality of work he or she does.

Weather Woes

You know the old expression, "Into every life a little rain must fall." When it comes to running a landscaping business, a little rain, a blizzard in April, or an El Niño that stirs up a freak tornado can seriously hamper your business operations and put you behind schedule. Naturally, all you can do is wait out inclement weather and catch up on office administration tasks like billing and cold calling. On days when you find yourself gazing out a window on a cold, drizzly vista instead of wielding a spade, devise a new schedule so you can catch up on the missed work as soon as possible. Never disappoint a customer—put in longer hours (as long as the light holds out) or work on weekends so you meet the demands of every job and the expectations of every customer in a timely manner. You could also make it a habit to overestimate the amount of time your jobs may take so you always have a little breathing room.

Sometimes weather will force you to play advisor to your customers. "Sometimes I have to tell customers when it's time to do certain jobs," says Collins. "For example, last fall I had a lot of customers who wanted their leaves raked. One kept putting off the job, so I encouraged him to do it sooner rather than later, because if I had waited until he wanted me to come out, there would have been three inches of snow on the ground."

Although many landscapers in northern climes choose to confine their business activities to the annual growing season and take a winter break, it is possible to run the business year-round by offering snow removal services. All it takes is a snow blade for your riding mower or truck and you'll be in business. Be sure to mention your snow removal services in all your promotional materials and on your website. It's also a good idea to do an extra mailing to your existing customers or to print fliers to remind people that you're just a phone call away.

See Figure 3–2 on page 46 for a list of hardiness zones and their average annual minimum temperature ranges.

USDA Hardiness Zones and Average Annual Minimum Temperature Ranges

Zone	Fahrenheit	Celsius	Example Cities
1	Below –50 F	Below –45.6 C	Fairbanks, Alaska; Resolute, Northwest Territories (Canada)
2a	–50 to –45 F	–45.5 to –42.8 C	Prudhoe Bay, Alaska; Flin Flon, Manitoba (Canada)
2b	–45 to –40 F	–42.7 to –40.0 C	Unalakleet, Alaska; Pinecreek, Minnesota
3a	–40 to –35 F	–39.9 to –37.3 C	International Falls, Minnesota; St. Michael, Alaska
3b	–35 to –30 F	–37.2 to –34.5 C	Tomahawk, Wisconsin; Sidney, Montana
4a	–30 to –25 F	–34.4 to –31.7 C	Minneapolis/St. Paul, Minnesota; Lewistown, Montana
4b	–25 to –20 F	–31.6 to –28.9 C	Northwood, Iowa; Nebraska
5a	–20 to –15 F	–28.8 to –26.2 C	Des Moines, Iowa; Illinois
5b	–15 to –10 F	–26.1 to –23.4 C	Columbia, Missouri; Mansfield, Pennsylvania
6a	–10 to –5 F	–23.3 to –20.6 C	St. Louis, Missouri; Lebanon, Pennsylvania
6b	–5 to 0 F	–20.5 to –17.8 C	McMinnville, Tennessee; Branson, Missouri
7a	0 to 5 F	–17.7 to –15.0 C	Oklahoma City, Oklahoma; South Boston, Virginia
7b	5 to 10 F	–14.9 to –12.3 C	Little Rock, Arkansas; Griffin, Georgia
8a	10 to 15 F	–12.2 to –9.5 C	Tifton, Georgia; Dallas, Texas
8b	15 to 20 F	–9.4 to –6.7 C	Austin, Texas; Gainesville, Florida
9a	20 to 25 F	–6.6 to –3.9 C	Houston, Texas; St. Augustine, Florida
9b	25 to 30 F	–3.8 to –1.2 C	Brownsville, Texas; Fort Pierce, Florida
10a	30 to 35 F	–1.1 to 1.6 C	Naples, Florida; Victorville, California
10b	35 to 40 F	1.5 to 4.4 C	Miami, Florida; Coral Gables, Florida
11	Above 40 F	Above 4.5 C	Honolulu, Hawaii; Mazatlan, Mexico

FIGURE 3–2: **USDA Hardiness Zones**

Mowing Down the Competition

N ow that you have a good idea of exactly what a lawn service operator or landscaper does, it's time to lay the groundwork for creating an efficient and successful business. The place to start on the quest toward establishing your business is with market research and doing a little daydreaming.

You have to have a dream to aspire to, especially in the beginning when you're struggling to build your customer base and income. There are some questions to ask yourself before you can envision what kind of service provider you'll be. Lawn and landscaping service providers differ greatly in their styles and reputations.

Tiger Time Lawn Care in Memphis, Tennessee, offers two unique services that make them stand out from the crowd. One is free lawn care to those who qualify and have a family member in the military serving in a combat zone. The other is the option to have lawns mowed by bikini-clad beauties. While we're certainly not suggesting you perform business services in your swimsuit, we are encouraging you to get creative and stand out from the crowd. Will you offer the best snowplowing contract in the Midwest, complete with holiday light-hanging services? Will you be known for your total xeriscaping makeover packages? Will you be an organic provider offering child- and pet-safe fertilizer and pesticide treatments? Maybe you'd just like to be the best basic lawn mowing service in your community and leave it at that.

Go online and take a look at these green businesses to get a feel for how they differ from one another: www.joshlandscape.com, www.cleanairlawncare.com, www.arbor-nomics.com, and www.lawncareboise.com. While you're perusing, make a list of what you like about each one.

Market research is necessary for several important reasons. First, it helps identify exactly who might be interested in using your services. Second, it helps determine whether the area where you want to set up shop can actually sustain your business. Finally, it

▶ Mission Possible

Understanding your market and the people you'll serve is critical to the success of your business. But understanding yourself and defining exactly what you plan to do is equally important. So follow the lead of America's most successful corporations and write a simple mission statement that includes your company's goals and outlines how you will fulfill them.

Here are three mission statement samples:

▶ "Jim's Mow, Rake 'n' Snowblow will serve the needs of busy urban professionals by providing year-round basic mowing, power raking, and snow removal. My goal is to land 15 steady, weekly customers in the first six months of operation with an aggressive, door-to-door marketing blitz, offering great deals."

► Mission Possible

► "Earth Horizons is a full-service lawn care provider that offers organic soil treatments, low emissions maintenance, and education on organic gardening for its clients. Courteous, prompt customer service, as well as knowledge of and certification in the application of organic pesticides, herbicides, and fertilizers, are hallmarks that will distinguish this business and allow it to achieve sales of $50,000 next year."

► "Sharp Yards is a full-service landscape and lawn care service provider offering more services than area major competitors. Sharp Yards' own employees provide these services, rather than outside contractors. This one-stop-shop approach combined with high quality craftsmanship and professionalism will help us reach our goal to be thought of as the best in our community."

Here are some actual mission statements from green industry business owners:

► "We're building our reputation one yard at a time."

► "To give a value-added service to our customers so they keep us and become a valuable part of our business."

► "Treat everyone's property like it was our own."

Finally, here's a longer, more encompassing mission statement from an actual business:

"Our mission at Celtic Lawn & Landscape, LLC, is to offer customers the highest quality of service and distinguish ourselves in the minds of our customers as the very best lawn and landscape company in the Metro Detroit area. The primary objective of Celtic Lawn & Landscape is to satisfy our customers, because without satisfied customers, our company would not exist. We believe our customers will respond positively to us when we provide and deliver outstanding service. We at Celtic Lawn & Landscape, LLC, are dedicated to this philosophy."

Your mission statement is your compass as well as the foundation on which your future is built. It can be one sentence long (as in the case of Pepsi's mission statement—"Beat Coke"), or it can be several paragraphs. The length doesn't matter; the direction it provides is what's important.

Use the "Mission Statement Worksheet," Figure 4–1, on page 50 to help flesh out your company's philosophy.

Mission Statement Worksheet

Begin by asking yourself the following questions:

Why do I want to start a lawn care business? _____

_____

What are my personal objectives? How do I intend to achieve them?

_____

What skills do I bring to the business that are useful and beneficial?

_____

What is my vision for this business? _____

_____

Where do I think I can take it in one, two, and five years? _____

_____

Using this information, write your mission statement here:

Mission Statement for (your company name)

_____

_____

_____

_____

_____

FIGURE 4–1: **Mission Statement Worksheet**
Here's your opportunity to try your hand at writing your own mission statement.

provides useful information and data that can help you avoid problems down the road that could negatively impact or destroy your business.

You might be thinking, "Whoa! I'm an aspiring lawn technician, not a statistician. Besides, people have lawns everywhere. There's bound to be enough business in my area to keep me busy."

Your success will be determined by the research you arm yourself with. The importance of staying informed on the current status of your industry is a survival skill, as illustrated in the following findings. According to *Irrigation and Green Industry* (IGIN) magazine, the U.S. green industry of lawn and landscape maintenance, landscape contractors, and architects generated $65 to $68 billion as of 2015.

IGIN's 2015 status report says, "A new group of contractors has entered the market . . . They sell a suite of services for complete landscape care but with an environmental edge. They offer integrated pest management, controlling invasive plants and insects through organic or mechanical methods. They mow lawns and trim shrubs with battery-operated equipment, or mowers using alternative fuels. This is a fast-growing segment of the market today." Eco-friendly, water sustainable, and "going green" related services are attracting both contractors and manufacturers.

Staying current on the industry as a whole is just part of what your knowledge base should be. The reality is that not every part of the country has the same need for green service providers. Take, for instance, those parts of the Southwest where the ground cover consists mostly of scrub, rocks, and lizards. Unless you're planning to install lava rock, cacti, or other drought-resistant plants, it's a safe bet that a traditional lawn care business is going to die on the vine. Likewise, even in states like Washington and Oregon, where rain is plentiful and the grass gets as high as an elephant's eye, it's possible to have an overabundance of lawn care and landscaping services in a particular area.

The best way to find out about these kinds of shortcomings—as well as potential opportunities—is by researching your target market. Fortunately, this is something you can undertake yourself even if you don't have a background in statistics or research, according to David L. Williams, Ph.D., former dean of the school of business administration at Wayne State University in Detroit.

"With the exception of questionnaire development, which can be difficult for a beginner to do well, you can pretty much handle all the research yourself on a reasonably small budget," Williams says. "The problem is, many small-business owners view market research as an optional expense. But it's the only accurate way to find out what's important to your customer."

This chapter will show you how to find out who will use your services, learn where they live and work, and determine the kinds of services they'll want you to provide. Armed with this information, you'll be able to make informed decisions that can help your business grow and prosper.

Defining Your Market

So who is the typical lawn care or landscaping customer? If you had to come up with a simple formula for defining your target audience for a green industry business, here's what it might look like:

Homeowners + Yards + Your Creativity = Potential Customers

If only it were that simple. There's a lot more to starting this kind of business than gleefully buying mowers and power tools, printing up business cards, and waiting for the phone to ring off the hook. You have to study the demographics of the area in which you wish to do business carefully so you can tailor your services to a specific niche within that market.

Demographics are the characteristics of the people in your target audience. These characteristics may include age, education and income level, gender, type of residence, and geographical location.

City-Data (www.city-data.com) holds a goldmine of this kind of information and is free. Just enter the town and state you'd like to know about and you get a full, current report on factors like median income, age, and sex of occupants; mean prices of housing units; what types of dwellings residents occupy; most common industries and occupations of residents; and detailed weather charts.

According to research by *Lawn & Landscape*, two-thirds of homeowners believe in lawn care but do it themselves. While that may seem on the surface to reduce the market to the remaining one-third homeowners, *Lawn & Landscape* points out that what it also means is that a lot of homeowners understand the benefits of the services you offer. They also point out that 74 percent of those surveyed who had fired their lawn care contractor did it because they were frustrated with the quality of work. *Lawn & Landscape* believes the reason actually points to the need for better communication and managing customer expectations to ensure satisfaction.

That takes in a lot of ground, so to speak, but if you look closely, you'll see there's a lesson there. To apply it, start by looking at the community where you want to establish your business. Maybe you live in a college town that's overrun with hale and hearty 18- to 20-year-old men. Maybe you live in a small town where the average wage is $20,000. Or maybe you live in a condo-heavy area. Maybe you should find somewhere else to set up shop. This is where the importance of detailed demographic and market research comes in.

Conducting Market Research

The goal of your market research is to touch base with potential customers to find out whether they'd be interested in using the services of a lawn care or landscaping business, as well as exactly what types of services they may require.

There are two kinds of research—primary, which is information gathered firsthand, and secondary, which is information culled from external sources. Each has its own merits as well as costs.

Primary Research

The most common forms of primary research are direct-mail surveys, telemarketing campaigns, and personal interviews. Assuming that you'll want to save your startup capital for equipment and advertising, you should probably try a survey first since it's the most cost-effective way to gather information. You also should do the survey yourself rather than hiring a market research firm, because that can be quite expensive.

Your survey can either be online or actual and should be no more than one page (or screen), since it's difficult to get busy people to fill out anything lengthier. The questions should be well phrased so they're direct, clear, and unambiguous. They also should be constructed so the information they gather is useful and conducive to analysis. For example, a question like "Would you be interested in hiring a lawn or landscape service?" isn't very useful because it's closed-ended, meaning it's possible for the respondent to give a yes or no answer without elaborating. That's not going to give you much insight, which is the whole point of this exercise.

Although you could draft the questions yourself, you should consider asking someone experienced in market research for help. Since market research firms tend to be pricey, Williams of Wayne State University suggests contacting the business school at your local university instead. A marketing professor on staff might be willing to draft your questionnaire for $500 to $1,000, or may even assign your questionnaire as a class project free of charge, as Williams himself has done. You'll also find a market research letter in Figure 4–2, and a questionnaire in Figure 4–3, on pages 54 and 55 that you can use as guidelines.

warning

Mailing lists are purchased for one-time use. Lists are "seeded" with control names so the seller will know if you use the list more than one time. If you wish to use the entire list more than once, you'll have to ante up again. However, anyone who responds to that mailing can become part of your own mailing list.

Market Research Letter

PTERODACTYL LAWN SERVICE

5555 Park Avenue
Lincoln Park, Michigan 55555
www.pterodactyl.com

July 5, 20XX
Mr. Rainer Sell
5555 Penny Lane
Plymouth, Michigan 55555

Dear Mr. Sell:

I'll bet after a long day at work, you're ready to stretch out in your recliner with the newspaper or the remote control and just relax and unwind. What you probably don't want to do is to spend a big part of your evening or weekend trying to whip your lawn into picture-perfect shape.

That's where I can help. I'm about to launch a lawn care service in the metropolitan Detroit area to take the burden off people like you who want a beautiful, healthy lawn, but have limited time to care for it. So would you please take a few minutes to answer the enclosed questionnaire to let me know if you might be interested in lawn care services?

Thanks for your help.

Mike Kairis

Mike Kairis, Owner
Pterodactyl Lawn Service

FIGURE 4–2: **Market Research Letter**
Tailor this letter for your market research needs.

Market Research Questionnaire

1. What is your age?
   ❏ 18–29   ❏ 30–45   ❏ 46–60   ❏ 61 and up

2. Which of the following lawn services might interest you? (Check all that apply.)
   ❏ Weekly mowing, edging, and trimming
   ❏ Hedge trimming
   ❏ Tree trimming
   ❏ Fertilizer application
   ❏ Pest control
   ❏ Winter snow removal

3. Is there any outdoor maintenance service we haven't mentioned that you'd like
   help with and if so, what? _____

4. What is the maximum you'd be willing to pay for basic mowing service?
   ❏ $25 per week   ❏ $40 per week   ❏ more than $40 per week
   ❏ Other (specify) $ _____ per week

5. Do you currently use a lawn care service? _____
   If no, would you consider using a lawn care service at this time? ❏ Yes   ❏ No

6. What is your household income?
   ❏ $25,000–$40,000   ❏ $41,000–$55,000
   ❏ $56,000–$70,000   ❏ $71,000 and up

7. What is your educational level?
   ❏ High school diploma   ❏ College degree   ❏ Graduate school degree

8. What is your profession? _____
   If you would like to be contacted by a lawn care service provider, please provide
   your name and phone number here: _____

   Thank you for your time.

FIGURE 4–3: **Market Research Questionnaire**
Here's a questionnaire you can use to round up your market data.

Surveying the Market

This part is easier than you might think. Start by purchasing a mailing list that's targeted to the market you wish to reach. Local homeowners associations, listing brokers, and even daily newspapers in major metropolitan areas can sell you a list of heads of households that can be sorted in many ways, including by zip code so you can target a specific geographic area. (You can find a huge listing of publications that sell their lists in the *Standard Rate and Data Service* directory, published by VNU, which can be found in many large libraries.) Some other criteria you're bound to be interested in will include occupation (if you're looking for homeowners with professional jobs), gender (according to a Harris Poll conducted for the National Association of Landscape Professionals in May 2015, men outpaced women when it came to hiring professional landscapers over the previous year), income (the more money someone makes, the more likely he or she will be willing to pay for lawn care and landscaping), and age (especially middle-aged people and senior citizens). Need another list source? Try the *Directory of Associations* (Gale Research), which can be found at most large libraries.

All of these groups were affected by the same economy, though. Think about services that would fill the needs found in the same Harris Poll mentioned above. Despite any economic concerns, 90 percent thought it was important to have a well-maintained yard.

One of the services you could add to your calling card that would address these needs is yard renovation. A redesign for food gardens or xeriscaping to cut water bills considers your customer's budgeting needs, but still requires maintenance by you.

Promoting yourself as a tutor and assistant who homeowners may call upon during the initial stages of their garden startups would be another way to go. You could offer a comprehensive money-saving tutorial that would cover landscape, hardscape, and lawn-keeping techniques. You could also take that opportunity to attach some of your other services to that. For example, the technology to harvest rainwater is still in its infancy, and the best time to cash in on a new trend is right when it starts. You can actually get certified with the American Rainwater Catchment Systems Association (www.arcsa.org).

tip ⓘ

Compiled lists are lists of names that have been culled from published sources such as telephone directories and organization rosters. Hot lists consist of the names of known buyers, and are usually taken from magazine subscription lists, mail-order buyer lists, and so on. Hot lists cost more to rent but are worth the cost because the information is usually fresher and more accurate.

Once you have your list in hand (which is usually priced as a flat rate per 1,000 names), you're ready to produce your questionnaire. If you're creating a hard-copy questionnaire, to keep the cost down, use your home computer to create your own letterhead and format the questionnaire, then stop by a quick print shop like FedEx Office and have it photocopied.

If you'd rather go virtual, you can use an online survey creator like Survey Monkey (www.surveymonkey.com) and email it. Survey Monkey is free for up to ten questions and 100 responses and includes customer support and pre-designed question styles. Their unlimited questions survey is $26 per month and lets you gather 1,000 responses per month, along with lots of additional extras.

Another good source of lists is consumer home and garden shows. The organizations that run these trade shows usually compile the names of attendees for their exhibitors. You may be able to purchase a copy of the list directly from the trade show organizer. You'll find a list of some of the largest lawn care and landscaping industry shows in this book's Appendix.

aha!

Visit your market area's county seat to obtain copies of census tracts, which give population density and distribution figures, as well as reports on population trends over the past ten years. Study the communities carefully for signs of declining, static, or small populations, since they're not likely to be hotbeds of new business prospects and may best be avoided.

Cash Bait

How would you like an easy way to improve your response rates? Try enclosing a crisp, new dollar bill with your survey. The dollar is sent as an advance token of thanks to the recipient for taking the time to fill out and return the questionnaire. Although it doesn't guarantee a response, the buck certainly is an attention-getter, and direct marketing studies have shown that sending even a small cash honorarium tends to improve the rate of return. This trick could cost you a pretty penny, since, according to Williams, surveys should be sent to a sample of at least 300 people to yield useful data. However, a sampling of even as few as 100 participants would be useful and only require a $100 investment if you choose to include a monetary incentive. You could also offer respondents a discount on your services in exchange for a completed questionnaire.

Calling All Lawn Owners

Telemarketing is a highly effective, if time-consuming, way to gather information. As with surveys, you'll need a strong telemarketing script with questions similar to those on your

▶ The Cream of the Crop

Upper-middle-class homeowners who hold white-collar jobs and own homes on 4,000- to 7,000-square-foot properties are usually the ripest prospects for lawn care and/or landscaping services, even if they already use such a service. They could be unhappy with the level of service they're currently receiving and may be receptive to a quote from you.

Be on the lookout for new subdivisions with estate-sized lots that are being built in your market area. Put on a company shirt and a dazzling smile, and make a point of visiting the new homeowners shortly after they move in—even if they don't even have their sod and landscaping installed yet. The landscaping company that lays the sod may have its own lawn maintenance division and certainly will make a bid to care for the lawn after the installation job is completed. So you'll want to make your own bid as soon as possible, since it's likely to be lower than that of an established landscaping business and thus may look very tempting to a cash-strapped new homeowner.

market research questionnaire and a good prospect list. But when you call, don't just fill out the form as the homeowner talks. Listen carefully to the person. He or she is bound to make comments and have concerns about things you never even considered. That helps you add to the storehouse of knowledge you'll tap into when you're ready to go after your first clients.

A Job for the Pros

If you're really nervous about doing your own market research and have a sufficiently large startup budget, you could hire a market research firm to help you. These firms are located in most large cities and will be listed in the Yellow Pages (www.yellowpages.com), or you can generically search the internet for market research firms. Not only will they collect information for you, but they'll also handle all incoming data, analyze the results, and prepare a report for your review.

However, hiring a marketing service can take a pretty big bite out of your startup budget (to the tune of a few thousand dollars for a few hundred interviews), so you'll want to seriously consider doing your own research before turning to the pros.

save

Try to keep the market area you serve within about five miles of your home (or office, if you go that route). Driving longer distances is costly in terms of time lost, money spent on gas and maintenance, and extra vehicle wear and tear.

Secondary Research

If you're looking for real cost savings when doing market research, try using secondary research. Someone, somewhere has probably researched something that relates to what you want to know, and you can often get your hands on that information free of charge.

The mother lode of statistical information can be found at state and federal agencies, since they collect data on everything from income levels to buying habits. Although this data may be a year or two old, it can still be very useful, particularly for the fledgling lawn or landscaping business owner who doesn't have a lot of money to spend on research. Some great sources of information are the U.S. Census Bureau (http://census.gov), the Small Business Administration (www.sba.gov), local economic development organizations, and even utility companies, which often have demographic data they'll provide free of charge or for a very nominal fee.

Other sources of useful secondary research include your local library, chamber of commerce, state economic development department, trade associations, and trade publications. You can find the names of thousands of trade publications in the *Standard Rate and Data Service* directory.

Economic Environment

Before we move on, there's one more very important factor to consider in your market research efforts. That's the economic base in your prospective market area.

Depending on what's happening with the national economy, a lawn care or landscaping service may be considered more of a luxury than a necessity. So it's up to you to convince your prospective clients that they need your services because it will make their lives easier.

If you've done your market research right, you already have some idea about the average income levels in your neighborhood. Now you need to look at data such as the percentage of people who are employed full time and the types of jobs they hold. If the local market is driven by a lot of blue-collar, heavy-industry jobs, a downturn in the economy could make cash tight and affect your ability to keep customers. So could a plant shutdown or a scaling back of local services. A call to your city's economic development office is an easy way to get a handle on the health of local industry. Ask about the area's white-collar jobs since these people are your best customer prospects, as well as the types of companies that employ them. You also need to make sure you have a backup survival plan if you aspire to serve an area that's heavily dependent on a single industry.

One lawn care business owner in Texas studied his market carefully before deciding to expand his lawn chemical services into a second market area. "My partner and I looked at demographics carefully because we were primarily interested in serving dual-income families with kids who had a minimum salary of $50,000," he says. "We figured these were our most likely prospects because they were busy and would want to enjoy their family instead of working on their yards."

It was a good call. His business grew nicely, thanks to door-to-door marketing efforts and postcard mailers.

Florida landscaper Mike Rosenbleeth used a similar approach. He targeted the owners of homes ranging in size from 2,000 to 3,000 square feet, or "the people you would expect would want to have the landscaping done for them," he says. As a result, he garnered 109 customers in the first five years of doing business—and the numbers continue to grow.

Your
Budding
Business

Just like grass seed needs nutrient-rich, fertile soil in which to grow, your lawn care or landscaping business needs a formal legal foundation to ensure compliance with commonly accepted business practices. This chapter discusses standard operating procedures for everything from naming your business to legal issues, and shows you how to get your business machine oiled, cranked up, and ready to run.

Naming Your New Baby

Choosing a name for your company should be high on your list of priorities in the early stages of business development. Many lawn service and landscaping business owners opt to use their own names combined with a business description, like "Elly's Lawn Care" or "Ted Jones Landscaping." There are a couple of advantages to this kind of name. Naming the business after a real person (that's you) can make the business seem more credible and reliable. It's also beneficial because many people like dealing with a company owner. A disadvantage to doing this is that if you ever sell your business, someone else will be operating under your name. Should you desire to start up another business with your name, there could be legal problems and confusion.

If you decide to use your own name, be sure to open a business checking account right away so you can keep careful records of business deposits and expenditures separate from your personal transactions. Otherwise, you could run into trouble at tax time because the folks in Washington may have trouble distinguishing between your personal income and your business income.

Colorado franchiser and landscaper Kelly Giard's business name lets potential customers know what they'll be getting with the name Clean Air Lawn Care. Mark Wise and Lindsay Stame feel that the name of their Illinois landscape business, Greenwise, sometimes doesn't beckon high-end jobs with its down-to-earth ring. They wanted their name to reflect that organic lawn care isn't a luxury service and is available for everyone.

Michigan landscaper Michael Collins chose to name the business he co-owns—Celtic Lawn & Landscape—after his Irish heritage rather than using his name. "We wanted to make the business stand out as professional, instead of sounding like a bunch of guys running around with our shirts off," he says. "Not that we would do that anyway—we wear uniforms."

Steve Mager, the owner of a lawn care business in Mendota Heights, Minnesota, has been grappling with

tip

Business checking accounts at large banks may come with hefty service fees. To find a small business-friendly bank, call around and compare fees before depositing your hard-earned cash. Another way to tell if the bank will appreciate your business: Visit www.entrepreneur. com/bestbanks for a state-by-state listing of the nation's small business-friendly banks.

the problem of name recognition since 1998, when he bought a full-service lawn care business that had been around for a decade. In his case, the previous owner's name wasn't part of the business name, but the positive reputation that he wanted to perpetuate did ride along with the business moniker.

"Even after all these years, I'm still not sure I like the name [The Cutting Crew], but other people seem to," says Mager. "I've been going back and forth about changing the name, but it's familiar to other people and it's catchy, just like you want a business name to be."

Mager's right. Catchy, creative names that identify who you are without being too cute can be great attention getters. But be sure to stay away from names that are too over-the-top, like "The Green Guy," "The Brawny Lawnman," or "Lawn Shark" (definitely too much like "Loan Shark"). Not only are overly cute names unprofessional, they won't inspire confidence in your clientele, either.

Nathan Bowers, a business owner in Sykesville, Maryland, learned this lesson firsthand. When he started his business as a teenager, he had a young man's enthusiasm for the wacky and fun. So he named his business "Yardvark," a deliberately misspelled variation on "aardvark." As both he and his business matured, he realized a name change was needed.

"I always got a lot of grief from customers, and after a while, even I started feeling foolish answering the phone 'Yardvark!' every day," says Bowers. "The name just didn't have a professional, commercial sound." So Bowers eventually renamed the business Premier Lawn Services, Inc., which has a more solid, dependable connotation.

By now it should be obvious that you should take your prospective business name out for a spin before you print up your business cards and other business documents. Have a friend call you a few times so you can answer the phone using the new name. It should roll off the tongue easily (just imagine saying, "Leonard Wisniewski Landscaping and Lawn Care" a couple dozen times a day). Be careful, too, if you pick names that use alliteration ("Steady Stu's Lawn Service") or use words that are hard to distinguish over the phone ("Tuck's Sod and Stuff").

There's another little trick you can use when selecting a name that can put your business in the spotlight immediately. Selecting a name that starts with an A or another letter toward the beginning of the alphabet can put you first in the phone business listings, which is helpful since people tend to start at the top of the listings when using a phone directory. Of course, not everyone can be listed in that coveted first spot (although some people just keep adding A's to their designation—like AAAAAAAA Lawn Service—to keep a stranglehold on first place), but you can choose a unique name that's distinctive and evocative of what your business does. To help you get started, check the Yellow Pages (www.yellowpages.com) for ideas (as well as to avoid duplication), then use "The Name Game" brainstorming form in Figure 5–1, pages 64 and 65.

The Name Game

Establishing a unique business identity is not just important; it's absolutely essential so prospective clients (and, alas, the IRS) can find you easily. Although it's quite common for lawn service owners to use their own names in their company monikers, that's not your only choice. Try completing the following brainstorming exercise to explore other possible name choices that can either stand alone or be combined with your own name.

List the top three things that come to mind when you hear the word "grass" (such as adjectives like "perfect" or "manicured," or nouns like "carpet"). Be creative!

1. _____

2. _____

3. _____

Now list synonyms for the words you just wrote down. If you need some creative ideas go to www.thesaurus.com and get access to descriptive words you may never have thought of. Make sure that they aren't so obscure that your audience won't get the gist of your business.

1. _____

2. _____

3. _____

List three unique landmarks or features that characterize the place where you'll do business (such as the abundant lakes in Michigan or the starkly beautiful Black Hills of South Dakota). CAUTION: Avoid weather references like "snow belt" or "desert" that will seem incongruous when combined with a lawn care reference!

1. _____

2. _____

3. _____

FIGURE 5–1: **The Name Game**

The Name Game

List three geographical references (such as your city, state, or regional area).

1. _____

2. _____

3. _____

Now, try combining elements from these four sections in different ways:

1. _____

2. _____

3. _____

Did you come up with something you liked? If not, try using alliteration or plays on words with any of the elements above to create an interesting business name.

Once you've selected a name, put it to the test:

❑ Say it aloud several times to make sure it's easily understood, both in person and over the phone. (Remember the name "Steady Stu's Lawn Service"? It has too many "s" sounds, making it too difficult to pronounce, let alone understand on the phone.)

❑ Do an online search to make sure someone else isn't already using the name you've chosen.

❑ Check with your county seat or other official registrar to make sure the name is available (since someone may have already claimed the name but may not be using it yet). If you plan on naming your website the same as your business name, check for domain availability at the same time at www.networksolutions.com.

Does your name pass the test? Congratulations! Now you're ready to register it.

FIGURE 5–1: **The Name Game,** continued

Once you've picked a suitable name, it's time to move on to the next step: Setting up your business structure.

Registering Your Corporate Name

Most states require you to register your fictitious company name to ensure that it's unique. This is usually done at the county level and is known as filing a dba ("doing business as") statement. The fee to file is usually nominal (around $30 to $60) and entitles you to use the name for a limited period of time—usually three years. When the time expires, you simply renew the dba. Before you get your dba, however, a search is done to make sure your name is unique. If you happen to choose a name that's already being used, you'll have to pick something else, so it's a good idea to have a few names in reserve.

Adding words to your actual name automatically makes it a fictitious name, which means you must register it. The good news is, unless you have a very common name (like John Smith), chances are it's unlikely to be in use already.

save

You can do your own no-cost name search online. Start by checking for nationally registered trademarks on the U.S. Patent and Trademark Office website at www. uspto.gov. You can also search for domain and business name availability through Yahoo!, Google, MSN, and Lycos.

Your Corporate Structure

Once you've registered your dba, you are considered to be the proud owner of a legitimate business. Naturally, the IRS will have something to say about the way you run it. (You knew we'd get around to the IRS eventually, didn't you?) Basically, this means the bureaucrats in Washington require that you operate as one of four business entities: a sole proprietorship, a general partnership, a limited liability company (LLC), or a corporation. Here's a brief look at each form.

Sole Proprietorship

Many lawn care and landscaping professionals choose to operate as sole proprietors because it's the easiest type of business to form. All you have to do is file a dba as discussed above, then open a business checking account in that name. You can use your personal credit card to pay for business expenditures if you want, and you'll still get tax benefits like business expense deductions. But there is a downside to the sole proprietorship. You are personally liable for any losses, bankruptcy claims, or legal actions that pertain to the business. That can wipe out both your personal and business assets if you're ever sued. (For this reason, good liability coverage is a must in this business. See Chapter 6 for a discussion of insurance options.)

General Partnership

If you're planning to join forces with another entrepreneur to open a business, you are forming a general partnership. Partnerships are easier to form than corporations, and you don't have to file any documents to make them legal. But since each partner is responsible for the actions of the other, it's a good idea to have an attorney draw up a partnership agreement that spells out exactly what each person is responsible for.

tip

BusinessUSA, www. business.usa.gov, offers a free, ten-step business startup guide and online tutorials for writing a business plan. Take advantage of this wealth of guidance from the experts.

Limited Liability Company

A third type of business entity is the limited liability company, or LLC, which combines the tax structure of a partnership with protection from personal liability. This type of partnership is a little less common among green industry professionals but can be useful if you want some added protection for your personal assets.

Corporation

The last type of business arrangement is the corporation. It is established as an entity that's totally separate from the business owner. Establishing a corporation requires filing articles of incorporation, electing officers, and holding an annual meeting. Not many lawn care professionals choose this option initially because the costs are prohibitive and the company must pay corporate taxes. On the other hand, owners of a corporation will find it easier to obtain financing for things like buying big-ticket equipment, building a storage facility, or buying property on which to put that storage facility.

If you operate under your own name, you can use your Social Security number when filing your business taxes. But if you adopt another name for your sole proprietorship as discussed earlier, or form a partnership or corporation, you are required to have a federal employer identification number (EIN). To apply for an EIN, pick up a copy of form SS-4 at any IRS office, or go to www.irs.gov where you can do it online. You'll also need a dba, as discussed earlier.

If you're not sure which business arrangement to choose, you should talk to an attorney experienced in handling small-business issues. "There are advantages to each kind of entity, and an attorney can help you decide which one is best for your situation," says attorney Daniel H. Minkus, past chairman of the business law section of the State Bar of Michigan and a member of the business practice group of Clark Hill PLC in Detroit. "If you don't know the people you are doing business with, I'd encourage you to form a single-member LLC or corporation. They're simple to create, and they're invaluable because your clients are dealing with your enterprise and not you personally."

You can incorporate without using an attorney. The forms are fairly easy to fill out, and it will cost you $50 to $300 to do it yourself, versus $400 to $1,000 if you have an attorney handle the process. But corporate law is complex, so it may be a better idea to allow a professional to handle this for you.

You'll find information about hiring an attorney in Chapter 6.

The Home Zone

Now that you're just about ready to start pounding the pavement for your first customers, it's time to investigate one last possible barrier to your business: your local zoning ordinances. These regulations can prohibit small businesses like yours from operating in certain areas, including residential neighborhoods. Such ordinances exist to protect people from excessive traffic and noise (as well as to rake in the extra taxes assessed on businesses). Because you won't have clients visiting your home, it's quite likely you can run the business quietly without anyone being the wiser. But if you intend to park a heavy-duty truck in your driveway that says "Ray's Mowing Service" on the doors, you'd better check with your local government office to see if any special permits are required for homebased businesses. It's better to find out upfront, before you go to the expense of printing stationery and obtaining a business telephone line, than to find out later that such businesses are prohibited.

Not every community will have a problem with equipment stored on your property, however. "I park a lot of vehicles in the driveway, so it looks like 'Beverly Hillbillies' around here," says one lawn care service owner in Washington state. "But we live in a remote area on the south end of an island, so no one has said anything . . . yet."

warning

Local governments (cities, townships, and counties) rather than states establish their own zoning regulations, and these regulations vary widely. A homebased business that's perfectly legal in one city could be verboten in another. The only way to find out is by calling the zoning board in your community.

Other Licenses and Permits

But wait, there's more! Some municipalities require the business owner to have a business license. It's usually available for a very nominal fee and is renewable annually.

If, by chance, you're turned down for a license because of zoning restrictions, you can apply for (and probably receive) a variance from the municipal planning commission so you can get your license.

If you're planning to use pesticides and other chemicals in your business, special licensing and certification are usually required. Requirements vary by state. Check with your state agriculture department for specifics on educational requirements, testing, and certification.

In addition, most states require lawn care and landscaping professionals to have other special licenses or permits. For guidance, you can contact:

▶ *The SBA.* Go to www.sba.gov.
▶ *Small Business Development Centers.* You can reach these through the SBA, or by logging on to www.sba.gov/tools/local-assistance/sbdc for a list of local offices.
▶ *SCORE.* Go to www.score.org. This nonprofit organization is an SBA partner and has hundreds of chapters throughout the United States.

For a bird's-eye view of licensing requirements by state, go to www.nationalcontractors.com/license.htm, where you'll also find links to each state's licensing website.

Navigating Unfamiliar Waters

There's one more task you have to complete before you can leave this chapter and plunge into the other uncharted waters that await you. This task can literally make or break your business. You have to write a well-thought-out, persuasive, and comprehensive business plan that will guide you and show potential investors and lenders that your intentions are logical and researched.

Your business plan is like a road map. It outlines your plans, goals, and strategies for making your business successful. It's useful not just for applying for credit or attracting investors, but for giving you direction so you can achieve even your loftiest goals as well as measure the success of your business over time. Without it, it's unlikely anyone will give you the capital you need.

stat fact

President Obama signed the Small Business Jobs Act in September 2010, creating powerful opportunities for entrepreneurs. The law puts more capital with enhanced loan provisions and higher loan limits into the hands of the small-business owner. It also creates federal contracting opportunities and expands training and counseling resources for small businesses. Read more about the billions in lending opportunities, tax cuts, and other opportunities here: www.sba.gov/jobsact.

There are seven major components every business plan should have. Here's how those elements apply to a lawn care or landscaping business:

1. *Executive summary.* In this section, which summarizes the entire business plan, you'll want to describe the nature of your business, the scope of the services you offer (mowing, fertilizing, pest control, irrigation, etc.), the legal form of operation (discussed earlier in this chapter), and your goals. If you expect to use the business plan to seek financing for your company, you should include details about your overall plans, too.

2. *Business description.* In the business description section, you'll describe both the lawn care or landscape industry and your target market. (You'll find general statistics about these industries in Chapters 2 and 3.) But for even more information that can prove helpful in establishing the viability of your business, check the Small Business Development Center website at www.sba.gov/tools/local-assistance/sbdc.

3. *Market strategies.* Here's another place where all that market research data you've collected will come in handy. In this section, discuss exactly what you'll do to reach customers and how you'll pull it off. Focus, too, on the things that make your company unique, like your knowledge of Feng Shui landscaping. You'll find more information about marketing plans in Chapter 10.

4. *Competitive analysis.* If you've done your homework well, you already know how many lawn care and landscaping businesses are operating in your target market. But in this section, you should also note other potential competitors, such as snow removal companies that do lawn care during the off-season, lawn and garden stores that have maintenance services, and even homeowners who choose to tend their own lawns or install their own shrubbery. Analyze their strengths and weaknesses, and contrast them against what you consider to be your own strengths.

5. *Design and development plan.* Here's where you'll consider how you'll develop market opportunities to help your company prosper and grow. It's helpful to create a timetable of objectives that you can look back on to benchmark your successes, like setting a goal for graduating from servicing 20 customers a week to 40, widening your service area to include a second community, or adding underground sprinkler installation to your service mix. You should also consider how much full- or part-time help you'll need to accomplish these lofty goals.

6. *Operations and management plan.* You can use the information in Chapters 2 and 3 of this book as a guide for this section, which discusses the day-to-day operations of your lawn care or landscaping business. You should create a simple organizational

chart—unless, of course, you're the only one on it; then it's not necessary. You also need to include a list of your overhead expenses, which include all the non-labor expenses you'll accrue, including office expenses like utility bills and office supplies, and business expenses like gasoline for your truck, mower blade sharpening, and supplies like trash bags and fertilizer. You should keep this section updated to reflect any new or expanded services you offer.

7. *Financial factors.* Even if you're a sole proprietor with very modest first-year expectations, you need to forecast the success of your business. This will help keep your business on track and help you avoid nasty surprises. Probably the most important document in this section should be your balance sheet, which will provide a running tally of how well the business is doing. You'll also need an operating income/expense statement, which is something we'll talk about in Chapter 13.

Constructing such a detailed business plan probably sounds like a lot of useless, boring work. After all, all you really need to do your job is a truck, a lawn mower or landscaping tools, and a dry day, as well as some space in your den or on your dining room table for doing paperwork or designing landscapes. But embarking on a new business without a clear-cut plan is like sailing for Europe without a navigational chart or a compass. Without a plan, you won't have any idea to whom you're selling your services or what they're even interested in. So take the time to formalize your business plan now, and refer back to it periodically for both inspiration and direction. You also should revise your plan periodically. For example, if you're not earning as much as you'd hoped, you might need to adjust your prices or delay equipment purchases. Adjust your business plan to reflect changes like these.

Finally, to keep track of all the details you need to juggle to get your new business revving, use our "Startup Checklist" in Figure 5–2, page 72.

Startup Checklist

❑ Select a business name with the help of the form in Figure 5–1, page 64.

❑ Apply for a dba.

❑ Decide on the best legal form for your business.

❑ Check local zoning regulations to make sure your business will be in compliance.

❑ Apply for a variance if zoning regulations prohibit you from running a home-based business.

❑ Apply for a business license if required in your community.

❑ Write your business plan.

❑ Contact an accountant to discuss the financial and tax requirements related to establishing and operating a business.

FIGURE 5–2: **Startup Checklist**

Use this checklist to keep on top of all the tasks you need to complete to get your new business up and running.

Cutting-Edge Help

J ust as a busy homeowner is happy to turn over the manicuring of his or her property to you, you'll want to relinquish some of the details of running your business to other professionals who have the expertise to do the job right. After all, even if you have the knowhow to do your own taxes or review a real estate lease, this isn't necessarily a good use of your time. It's almost always better to spend the lion's share of your working hours on the activity you do best—lawn care or landscaping—and rely on other professionals to keep your business humming along behind the scenes.

This chapter will give you insight into why you should consider hiring an attorney, an accountant, and an insurance agent, as well as discuss what you can expect them to do for you.

Your Legal Eagle

You're reliable and prompt, conscientious and professional. So you couldn't possibly ever have to worry about being sued by one of your friendly, long-standing clients, right?

Wrong.

Unfortunately, whenever a job involves working with the public, the potential to be sued exists. The lawsuit could be over a matter that you couldn't possibly

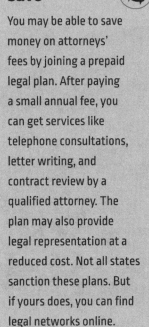

save

You may be able to save money on attorneys' fees by joining a prepaid legal plan. After paying a small annual fee, you can get services like telephone consultations, letter writing, and contract review by a qualified attorney. The plan may also provide legal representation at a reduced cost. Not all states sanction these plans. But if yours does, you can find legal networks online.

have controlled, like lightning striking the lawn mower you left under the cover of a weeping willow during a thunderstorm, which caused an electric jolt to travel up the trunk and split it in two. Or you could even be sued by one of your own employees who got hurt on the job.

It makes sense to retain an attorney before anything ever goes wrong so you have someone to turn to for advice and guidance if and when the time comes.

Following is a list of some of the reasons a lawn care or landscaping professional might hire an attorney:

- ▶ You want to form a partnership or a corporation.
- ▶ You find the language in a contract difficult to understand.
- ▶ You're signing a contract for a lot of money or one that will cover a long period of time, such as an expensive equipment purchase or a long-term lease on an office site.
- ▶ You're being sued or someone is threatening to sue you.
- ▶ You need help with tax planning, loan negotiations, employee contracts, and other matters.

"But above all, protecting yourself from liability is one of the most important things you must do as a small-business owner," says Daniel H. Minkus, a Michigan attorney.

▶ A Match Made in Heaven

Just as every lawn care or landscaping business owner is different in terms of his or her personal style, temperament, and experience, attorneys are different from one another. The trick is to find a lawyer who meets your personal needs and expectations, and whose strong communication skills make him or her easy to talk to. Here are some general questions to ask that can be helpful in determining whether your attorney-to-be is one you want to have and to hold:

- ▶ What is your background and experience?
- ▶ What's your specialty?
- ▶ How long have you been practicing?
- ▶ Do you have other small-business owners as clients?
- ▶ Have you ever represented a lawn care or landscaping service owner before?
- ▶ Will you do most of the work, or will a paralegal or other aide help out?
- ▶ Is there a charge for the initial consultation?
- ▶ What do you charge for routine legal work?
- ▶ Do you work on a contingency basis?

"An attorney can help you assess your risk for being party to a lawsuit and help you minimize it."

As you know from Chapter 5, establishing an LLC or a corporation is a good way to limit the liability on your personal property. Limiting your financial liability when hiring an attorney is just as important, especially when you're just starting out and your cash flow is modest.

Minkus says that because you don't need a litigator to handle the routine legal work, you can keep the cost down by hiring an attorney in a one- or two-person practice. Attorneys' hourly rates typically run from $150 to $450, with the higher rates being charged by senior partners and those who work at larger firms. Other factors that influence cost include geographic location, the experience of the attorney, and his or her area of expertise.

Because some attorneys charge an initial consultation fee, be sure to ask about it before you ever set foot in his or her office. In addition, you may have to pay your attorney a retainer upfront, which he or she will draw against as work is completed. Others charge a contingency fee, which means they take a percentage of any lawsuit settlement that's reached. Still others charge a flat fee for routine work, such as filing incorporation papers.

Another way to keep your legal costs reasonable is simply by being organized. "Do your own legwork to gather the information you need beforehand, and limit the number of office visits you make," Minkus advises. "You also should limit phone calls to your attorney, because you'll be charged for those, too."

Many attorneys offer startup packages that can be affordable for small-business owners. While you can often tailor such packages to meet your needs, they typically include an initial consultation, as well as all activities related to the LLC or incorporation process, including the filing of paperwork with your state and other corporate formalities. You can expect to pay approximately $500 if you're establishing an LLC, or about $900 if you're setting up a corporation. A payment plan may be available to help you handle the cost.

stat fact

The American Bar Association's Commission on Women in the Profession report "A Current Glance at Women in the Law, July 2014" shows that the Bar's market research department found that 34 percent of lawyers are women. A 2015 report from the Labor Force Statistics shows women at just 8.4 percent of the U.S. landscaping work force, a mere .2 percent increase from 2007.

Locating an attorney you like and respect is often as simple as asking friends or relatives for a referral. In any event, Minkus says getting a referral is much more reliable than just opening your internet search engine and picking someone at random. Another way to find a lawyer is through attorney referral services, which are located in many counties throughout the United States. You can contact the American Bar Association by visiting www.americanbar.org/aba.html, or visit www.martindale.com.

Money Managers

It's usually easier to convince new business owners that they need an accountant than to convince them they need an attorney. Most people are either admirably adept or totally clueless when it comes to budgeting, bookkeeping, and other financial matters. But even those who feel comfortable cranking out their personal taxes annually or investing online may blanch at the thought of creating profit and loss statements and other complex documents. That's usually a pretty reliable sign that you need to book the services of a professional accountant.

An accountant can help you establish an effective record-keeping system, keep expenses in line, and monitor cash flow. He or she also can advise you on tax issues, which is crucial because tax law is very complicated and changes frequently. (The IRS issues new tax rulings every two hours of every business day!) Tax issues that might be relevant to a lawn care or landscaping professional include the amount you can deduct annually for business expenses (including travel and office equipment) and the amount of money you can deposit to your retirement account annually.

Like an attorney, an accountant experienced in handling small-business tax issues also can advise you whether you should incorporate your business. In addition to protecting your personal assets, incorporating can cut your tax bill, allow you to put more money into your personal investments, and offer other useful benefits.

tip

Hiring an enrolled agent instead of an accountant can save you money if you're only looking for tax help. In addition to preparing your tax return, enrolled agents can represent you before the IRS. They can be found online through the National Association of Enrolled Agents (www.naea.org).

There are two types of accountants. Certified public accountants, or CPAs, are college-educated and have to pass a rigorous certification examination in the state where they do business in order to put those coveted letters after their names. Public accountants aren't certified and don't have to be licensed by the state. While they may be perfectly capable due to their experience, they usually can't represent you before the IRS if you're called in for an audit.

There's also a wide range of accounting software on the market that can help you crunch the numbers and manage your business accounting. QuickBooks is the choice of many lawn care and landscaping business owners. Keep in mind, however, that some of the other packages around may not satisfy IRS requirements for record-keeping. It's probably wiser to rely on a professional to handle accounting matters whenever you need to do anything more complex than record credits and debits or informally tally up business expenditures.

To find an accountant, ask your attorney, banker, or other business professionals you deal with for a referral. The American Institute of Certified Public Accountants' branch in your state also can refer you to a qualified number cruncher, or you can refer to its website at www.aicpa.org. It's very important to select someone who has experience either with small-business clients in general or lawn care or landscaping business owners in particular. Avoid accountants who specialize in large corporations, since they're not likely to be as familiar with small-business concerns as you'd like.

Accountants charge $75 to $125 an hour and up. You can keep your accountant's costs down by organizing your financial records and receipts before you meet (overflowing shoeboxes are not considered a viable accounting system!). You'll find more bookkeeping strategies and advice in Chapter 13.

Computing King

Lots of people know how to turn on and at least peck out a few commands on a computer these days, but when it comes to fixing a beeping, buzzing glitch or going to battle with the dastardly Blue Screen of Death, most of us are without a clue. For this reason, it's a good idea to add a computer consultant to your business management team. Computer consultants usually charge from $35 to $75 an hour, and can assist with those indecipherable bit and byte problems that arise. They also can do everything from reformatting your hard drive to maximize performance and installing new peripherals and software to helping you keep abreast of technological advances.

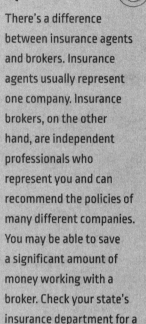

tip

There's a difference between insurance agents and brokers. Insurance agents usually represent one company. Insurance brokers, on the other hand, are independent professionals who represent you and can recommend the policies of many different companies. You may be able to save a significant amount of money working with a broker. Check your state's insurance department for a list of reputable brokers.

Be sure to choose a computer consultant who makes house calls so you can avoid having to disconnect all those mysterious cords and cables that run from the back of your computer to who knows where. Geek Squad technicians come to you and service many electronics besides just your computer. To find a branch near you, see www.geeksquad.com. You'll pay more for onsite visits, but it's worth it in the long run, both in terms of convenience and reduced aggravation.

Covering Your Assets

The other business professional you should have on your side is an insurance agent. Although you could use one of those online services that guide you to discount insurance brokers, it's usually better (and less time-consuming) to find an agent in your own community instead (or at least at the time of startup—you can comparison shop and switch later). This will allow you to discuss the particulars of your own business with an agent to make sure you're covered against all potential pitfalls. Face-to-face interaction is the best way to accomplish this. It's also the most reliable way for you to get adequate coverage. An experienced agent will be familiar with the risks you might encounter in your business and can recommend exactly how much coverage you need to protect yourself against those risks.

The easiest way to locate an insurance agent who can help you with your business needs is contacting the person who currently insures your home, apartment, or automobile. Alternatively, you can find agents by searching online.

Types of Insurance

Figuring out what kind of business insurance you need can be a dizzying proposition. Insurance is necessary for risk management because it's so easy to sustain a loss that could force you into bankruptcy. The trouble is, you can also go bankrupt trying to protect yourself against every possible situation that could result in litigious action. So in this section, we'll discuss some of the types of insurance you may need for your lawn care or landscaping business and let you decide for yourself which ones to spring for. Don't have a clue where to start? One reasonable way to approach the process is to decide how much of a loss you could personally afford to cover and buy insurance to offset the rest of the risk.

If you don't have an insurance agent, now's the time to find one, since he or she can help you muddle through this somewhat confusing—and expensive—purchase process. We also recommend looking for package insurance deals and obtaining cost estimates from at least two reliable agents since prices can vary so widely.

You need two types of insurance: insurance to cover the loss of or damage to your equipment, as well as injuries to employees, and insurance to cover damage to clients' lawns or property due to errors or negligence.

Here are the types of insurance that will cover these two situations:

▶ *Commercial general liability (CGL).* This type of insurance covers any kind of bodily injury, including injuries caused by employees operating a company vehicle, as well as property damage or loss, like if your lawn mower throws a rock through a customer's bay window. It also covers personal injury as a result of slander or damage to one's reputation, although this is not a common occurrence in the lawn care or land-scaping industry (unless you unfairly impugn another green industry professional's reputation and he or she decides to sue). You'll still need to supplement your CGL insurance with workers' compensation and auto insurance, but this policy is pretty comprehensive. In fact, most of the other types of insurance mentioned below are included

aha!

Try the Independent Computer Consultant Association to find a whole host of contractors who can set up your website at www.icca.org.

in the standard CGL policy. You can expect to pay $300 to $800 a year for $500,000 to $1 million worth of coverage.

▶ *Fire and general property.* This covers fire losses, vandalism, and weather-related damage, but it's only necessary if you own or rent a commercial building. Homebased businesses would purchase a business owner's policy instead (see "business owner's policy" below).

▶ *Fidelity bonding.* This is "honesty" insurance, so to speak, that protects businesses and their clients from financial losses due to dishonest employees. It's unusual for lawn care or landscaping businesses to be bonded, but some people consider it a sign of trustworthiness on the part of the business owner. (Just search online for services like plumbing to see how often the word "bonded" pops up.) You have to pay for bonding for every job you do, which will cost about $50 per job for a year's coverage. That means if you have 15 customers and you wish to be bonded for all of them, it will cost you $750.

▶ *Business-interruption.* This replaces business income and pays for expenses like equipment, office rent, etc., after a fire, theft, or other insured loss. This isn't a common stand-alone policy for lawn service or landscaping business owners, but it may be useful if you have a lot of expensive equipment you'd like to protect.

▶ *Business owner's policy (BOP).* This is a comprehensive package that provides general liability ($500,000 limit), fraud insurance, and business-interruption insurance for homebased businesses. This multi-insurance package is usually more affordable than buying separate policies and is an alternative to purchasing the CGL policy, which only covers personal injury and property damage. The average cost of a small-business owner's policy is $400 to $600 per year (www.insureon.com).

▶ *Business auto.* This is just the thing you need to cover your company truck. The costs vary widely depending on the number of vehicles you have, the type and size of the vehicle, where the vehicle is parked, the radius it's driven from home base, and the cargo it carries.

▶ *Workers' compensation.* This compensates employees for work-related injuries, diseases, and illnesses. Most states require employers to carry this type of insurance, and the cost varies by state. The state of Michigan, for instance, uses the "open competition" system, letting market forces set the rate by allowing companies to shop around. If you're lucky, you may be in a state that doesn't require workers' comp if you only have one employee (and by the way, you personally don't count as an employee). But even if you don't need workers' comp, you do need insurance against work-related injury lawsuits. Talk to an insurance agent for advice.

Business Insurance Planning Worksheet

Type	Required?	Premium
Commercial general liability		
Fire and general property		
Fidelity bonding		
Business-interruption		
Business owner's policy		
Business auto		
Workers' compensation		
Total Annual Cost		

FIGURE 6–1: **Business Insurance Planning Worksheet**
Plan what kind of insurance your business will need and how much it will cost with this worksheet.

Use the business insurance planning worksheet shown in Figure 6–1 to take notes on the different types of insurance coverage your business may need.

Tools of the Trade

N ow that you've got all that pesky administrative stuff out of the way, it's time to start thinking about the fun stuff—namely, the toys you'll need to run this grand enterprise of yours. If you've always had a love of and knack for caring for your own lawn, you may already have enough maintenance equipment to get your business off the ground. Of course, it's always more fun to go shopping for newer, bigger, more powerful equipment. After all, this is a serious business you'll be running, and serious businesses need serious tools. Plus, you may discover that the mower and other equipment you have parked in your tool shed may not be powerful enough for the daily punishment you're going to give it. This chapter will discuss the various tools you'll need to run the business and will help you take a systematic approach to estimating your startup costs so you know whether you need to seek outside financing.

Lawn Maintenance/Landscaping Equipment

The basics you need to get your business off the ground fall into roughly four categories: lawn maintenance and/or landscaping equipment, office equipment (including furniture and business machines like computers), office supplies, and business services. Check out Figure 7–1, pages 104 and 105, where we provide high- and low-end startup expenses for two hypothetical lawn care businesses. You'll find a worksheet in Figure 7–2, starting on page 106, which you can use to estimate and calculate your total startup costs in each of these four categories.

Vehicle

Your biggest expenditure by far for either a lawn care or landscaping business will be for the purchase of a sturdy, reliable vehicle for hauling your equipment if you don't already own a truck that can serve this purpose. Landscaping experts recommend choosing a heavy-duty flatbed truck (one-ton rated) with at least one locking toolbox ($200 and up) mounted on the flatbed and a dumping mechanism for unloading topsoil and other landscaping materials quickly and without shoveling (starting at $900). You'll find that a vehicle like the Ford F-150 with the optional trailer tow and snow plow prep package will run around $27,000; the Chevy Silverado 3500 Big Dooley with a crew cab long box and the optional trailer package has an MSRP of about $34,000; and a Silverado 2500HD diesel with a standard crew cab and trailer package will be stickered close to $36,500.

Eco-landscapers Marc Wise, Lindsay Stame, and Kelly Giard fuel their heavy-duty trucks with bio-diesel and plow in the winter. Of the $25,000 to $50,000 liquid capital Kelly recommends new entrepreneurs start their businesses with, roughly $15,000 to $20,000 of that should be set aside for the truck purchase and $5,000 to $10,000 for additional equipment. Michigan landscaper Michael Collins recommends purchasing a super-duty model if you're planning to plow because both plowing and towing can be hard on the front end. Even though Ford's F-150 pickup now comes with a plow prep option, it is intended for "light plowing," not that of someone doing it for a business. Of course, the payment on a $40,000 truck at 8 percent for five years would be $811 a month—a big liability for a startup business. So if you want to keep your costs down, scour the classifieds for a used vehicle instead.

After you've settled on a truck, make a beeline for the nearest sign shop and order a magnetic sign or decal with your company name and phone number. You can have a pair of custom signs (for both sides of your vehicle) made up for about $45. (See "Logo Design" in the Appendix for the names of businesses you can contact on the internet.) Decals cost even less but won't last as long. Although you'll probably want to leave your magnetic sign on the truck most of the time, you may find, as Florida landscaper Mike Rosenbleeth did, that there are times when you want to remove it. He takes his signs off when he goes to church but otherwise leaves them on. Once you have your signs, be sure to park your truck in a prominent place in front of your job sites to garner free publicity while you work. Consider creating several larger magnetic signs with funny, lawn-related sayings or helpful tips made and rotate their usage on your truck for attention. Keep it tasteful and classy!

tip

Carry a first-aid kit in your truck, complete with Benadryl® for multiple bee stings. Supply your workers each with one of their own for job sites. A nest full of angry hornets is one thing, but add a worker who didn't know he was allergic and you've got yourself a mess. Insist on preventative safety for your staff and set aside an hour a month for a quick breakfast and safety meeting. You can find the Easy Care First-Aid Kit at www.target.com for $24.99.

Utility Trailer

This is a must if you have a lot of equipment and don't want to be hoisting it up repeatedly into your van or truck bed. A new, steel mesh landscape trailer can cost $1,500 and up. A plain-Jane 5-by-10-foot single-axle light-duty trailer with 12-foot side rails and a ramp gate (also a must so you can wheel mowers aboard) starts at about $800 new. Check your local classified ads and our Appendix for new and used trailer resources.

Lowell Pitser in Stanwood, Washington, swears by the used boat trailer he bought for $150—with a boat still on it. "We had a nice bonfire in the front yard when we brought it home," he says, laughing.

The two most time-saving purchases for Marc Wise of Greenwise Organic Lawn Care were his chipper-shredder vacuum and his dump trucks. Imagine condensing all of the refuse you'll be carting off-site into a much, much smaller pile with a shredder. It's a good thing to think about when choosing your landscape trailer and will determine the style you decide on. You find them in the range of $1,500 to $7,000. Last but not least, invest in locking tie-downs to keep your equipment safe when you're on the road. Locking 8-foot tie-downs will run about $18 each.

Vehicle Alarm System

With all that expensive equipment you'll be hauling around to job sites, you might want to consider installing an alarm system on your vehicle. By far the most economical system is the alarm/kill switch combination. More than that probably isn't necessary. Perpetrators are more likely to try to swipe the whole rig rather than breaking in to steal individual tools or machines. Some vehicles come equipped with this feature, but if yours doesn't, you can shop for a security system on www.bestbuy.com and have it professionally installed by Best Buy partner Geek Squad.

Storage Facility

Just as you can work out of a home office, you can start your business without the overhead cost of a storage facility by using your own garage or shed. A shed kit with pre-

► A Truckload of Savings

Although it might be tempting to pick up a shiny new truck for your shiny new business, it's not always economically feasible for a startup small-business owner. So you should look into the possibility of purchasing a late-model pickup truck instead. A used vehicle is a better value because you'll save a lot on the purchase price, the insurance premiums may be lower, and you'll have lots of vehicles to pick from in your price range because there are so many off-lease vehicles.

Speaking of leasing, it's usually better to purchase than lease your vehicle. You'll be loading and unloading heavy equipment that will be covered with oil, grass clippings, and dirt, resulting in significant wear and tear on the vehicle. You can avoid the stiff penalties the leasing companies assess for excessive wear and tear when you buy instead. Chances are, it won't cost you much more to buy a used truck than it would to lease one. Local farm auctions, www.carsoup.com, and www.craigslist.org can yield great deals if you're an informed shopper.

cut, easy-to-assemble pieces can be delivered right to your door, or you can save money by purchasing plans for around $50 and building it yourself. Your neighbors are less apt to complain about a shed that's attractive and tidy looking. The cute, cottage-like sheds at Jamaica Cottage Shop start at around $3,000 plus delivery. See www.jamaicacottageshop. com for more information. Penny Pincher Barns (www.pennypincherbarns.com) offers plans and kits for attractive "barns" (sheds), garages, and carports for that shiny truck of yours. Check on what local building permits your town requires before purchasing. In addition to sheltering your vehicle, you'll want to use the space to do repairs and store equipment and extra supplies like trash bags and fertilizer. You can pick up heavy-duty industrial shelving for about $69 and standard utility shelving for about $25 at a home improvement store.

If you don't have enough room in your garage or carport, you'll have to find another facility because many cities have ordinances that prohibit parking commercial vehicles on residential streets overnight. An alternative to using your own garage would be to rent a bay in a self-storage facility. A space as small as 10 by 15 feet, which is about the size of a large bedroom, is sufficient for lawn equipment and miscellaneous supplies. If you want to park your truck inside, you'll need about 10 by 20 feet (a small one-car garage size), or 10 by 30 feet if you want to pull your trailer in, too. The rent varies widely according to which part of the country you live in, but you can expect to pay $50 to $200 a month.

Florida landscaper Mike Rosenbleeth leases 60 percent of a 5,000-square-foot warehouse located about 10 miles away from the customers he services. It's expensive—$1,200 a month (rents are generally high in Florida, he says)—but it's an ideal place to park one of the trucks, the three trailers, and the other equipment he uses. In addition, he uses 500 square feet of the space as an office where he holds crew meetings and handles office administration.

Uniforms and Hats

Apparel that bears your company name and logo creates as much visibility as the magnetic signs on your truck. Name recognition and association with quality happens when passersby notice how hard the crew wearing your name is working. Personalized T-shirts and hats not only give you a neat, professional appearance, but they also function as low-cost advertising tools. An added bonus is that the IRS actually considers shirts that have your company name and logo on them to be advertising and will allow you to deduct their cost. Other work clothes, including work pants or jeans and steel-toed shoes, are not deductible.

Embroidered polo shirts cost around $15 to $30 each, T-shirts cost around $13 each, and hats run about $12 to $17 each.

Safety Equipment

Anyone who works with power equipment should consider wearing ear protection. Lawn equipment operates at up to 95 decibels, and according to OSHA, hearing damage can occur with even limited exposure to sound levels in the 85-to-90-dB range. Earmuff-style hearing protectors that look like stereo headphones are affordably priced at around $25 a pair.

While you're at it, invest in a sturdy pair of safety glasses. They're getting more stylish all the time and they'll protect your eyes from rocks and other projectiles churned up by your mower or other equipment. They're a bargain at about $8 a pair.

You should also wear work gloves while on the job. They give you a firmer grip on the handles of your equipment, which is especially important when your hands are sweating in hot weather. Opt for inexpensive gloves—as long as they're reasonably durable—since they're so easily misplaced or lost. Gloves usually cost only a few dollars.

Steel-toed work boots are another important part of your workday ensemble. At an average of $90 a pair, they're on the steep side, but they can save you a world of hurt and prevent costly medical bills. Buy the best you can afford (they can cost upwards of $200), and make sure they have good arch support.

The final thing you should stock up on is sunblock. You're going to be in full or hazy sunlight every day you're on the job, and studies have shown that prolonged exposure to the sun (particularly during the peak hours of 10 A.M. to 3 P.M.) increases your risk of developing skin cancer, including deadly melanoma. No matter what your ethnicity is, you need a sunscreen with a minimum of SPF 45 to protect your skin. Don't forget to wear a hat (with your company logo, of course) to shield both your face and your scalp even after you've applied sunscreen.

tip

Create a free blog on WordPress (www.wordpress.com) to show off your expertise to loyal and potential customers. Review new landscaping tools and give money-saving tips and tutorials on keeping a rich-looking garden and well-fed lawn. Include lots of photos. If you link to other like-minded blog sites, they'll sometimes link back to you, expanding your readership. Do a search on the most popular "green," "landscaping," etc., bloggers and send them a short email, asking that they review your blog. You can offer local bloggers a chance to prove your quality by offering a coupon for one free lawn mowing, which should lead to a review.

Digital Camera

A digital camera really comes in handy for documenting projects and progress on job sites. Landscapers in particular often take before and after photos of their work, then post them on their website in a virtual portfolio or print them so they can be mounted in a portfolio that can be carried to design consultations.

You can get away with the heightened quality of today's smartphones to take your pictures; most even have telephoto and wide angle capabilities. But if you want to enlarge your photos to any degree and use them as printed images (as opposed to posting them online), you will want to have a digital SLR, which allows you to interchange lenses. Canon and Nikon make basic digital SLR cameras that run in the range of $500 if you want an extra lens or some accessories. With a USB cord, you can download your pictures directly from your camera to your laptop. If you order your camera online, make sure to read the product specs and suggested accoutrements.

You can use any inkjet printer to print your photos from your computer, although you may want to invest in a printer that's just for digital photos. These start at about $100, while the photographic paper costs $14 for 100 sheets of 8.5-by-11-inch paper and inkjet print cartridges are $30. Alternatively, you can take your photo media card to just about any drugstore and make prints using the digital photo printing machine. However, you're at the mercy of the person who runs the machine, so the quality may not always be as good as you'd like. There are still a few photo shops around that will print out high quality images for you.

Lawn Care Necessities

Let's get down to the nitty-gritty. To get started in the lawn care business, you'll need many pieces of equipment, not the least of which is a lawn mower. Some you may already have one at home; others you may need to purchase. Whatever the case, acquire equipment carefully and shop around. Keep in mind that the lowest price isn't always the best deal. Reading product reviews online will help you avoid pitfalls.

Lawn Mowers

There's a dizzying array of lawn mowers on the market. These days, most are self-propelled, a feature you'll greatly appreciate after you've spent hours crisscrossing acres of green grass under the blazing sun. Mowers often come with very useful attachments and features like mulchers and side catchers that can make your job easier. And for bigger jobs, a riding mower is a necessity. You will also definitely want a standard walk-behind model in your arsenal for hills and smaller jobs. Make sure you get a mower with a floating deck, if you plan on mowing hills. The decks float to hug turf contours and provide a beautiful, finished cut.

Since you're planning to make a go of lawn care as a business, invest in a good commercial mower rather than just using the one in your garage. Properly maintained, a commercial model can mow many lawns for years to come with minimal engine trouble. In contrast, the mowers you buy from your local discount or department store might only last for a single season, depending on how many lawns you mow. You can always use your nonprofessional mower as a backup if your primary mower needs servicing.

Commercial walk-behind lawn mowers come in widths from 21 to 60 inches. You can get a reliable mower for $1,000 to $2,600. Of course, you can spend even more if you want. For instance, a top-of-the-line 60-inch Exmark zero-turn-radius can cost $11,000! Some places sell off their demo models at a greatly reduced price, so keep tabs on your local dealers of the brand of mower you prefer. Like your truck or car, you usually can negotiate the price down when you buy from a dealer who specializes in lawn care equipment. In addition to Exmark, some well-known commercial equipment manufacturers include Husqvarna, John Deere, and Scag.

> **tip**
>
> Due to the growing number of consumers looking for earth-friendly businesses, push mowers are back in and solar mowers are growing in popularity for green industry service providers. Push mowers are now light and easy to use, not like the awkward and heavy monster your grandpa pushed around. Shop for enviro-friendly lawn care innovations here: www.peoplepowered machines.com, www.neutonpower.com, and www.husqvarna.com/us/homeowner/products/robotic-mowers/auto mower-solar-hybrid.

The warranties on commercial mowers (and other commercial equipment, for that matter) tend to be very short—as short as 90 days—because of the rough treatment they get. For that reason, it's usually not possible to buy an extended warranty. But some lawn equipment dealers do offer zero-downtime coverage at an extra cost so you have the use of a comparable loaner while your machine is in the shop. This type of policy costs a few hundred dollars a year and might be worth it if you're the cautious type.

Finally, before you can mow, you need to know exactly how much lawn you're working with so you can give an estimate to a prospect. A measuring wheel runs about $30.

Snow Removal Equipment

If you're planning to offer snow removal services in the winter, you'll need a snow plow for your truck or a snow blade for your lawn mower. Plow and blade styles and prices vary widely because they're scaled to the size of your machine, but a recent internet search turned up a new, steel $7^1/_2$-foot Western MVP Plus™ v-plow for $5,200 (including installation) and a used $7^1/_2$-foot Western UniMount Pro® snow plow with mount included, in good condition, for $1,200. A 16-inch riding lawn mower snow blade like the Craftsman® 24414 is about $450 new. You can even find blades and plows on eBay, but because of their weight, you'll want to pick them up in person from the seller. (Bring a forklift to get them into your flatbed.)

tip

It's essential to clean your lawn mower deck frequently during the mowing season. Not only will a simple cleanup keep the mower performing at peak condition, but you'll also prevent the spread of lawn diseases like powdery mildew and rust, two common types of lawn fungi.

Spreaders and Sprayers

Even if your intent is to stick to mowing, it's a good idea to offer fertilizing as one of your basic services. For that, you'll need a broadcast granular spreader, which, as the name implies, disperses the fertilizer in a wide arc. Spreaders cost around $35.

To attack weeds growing in cracks in the sidewalk or driveway, invest in a small, three-gallon pressurized herbicide sprayer. It will run about $40. If you're working on properties larger than half an acre, the four-gallon backpack sprayer is your best bet to ease the weight. Those are about $70.

The Final Four

You'll need four more pieces of commercial equipment to groom your customers' lawns to perfection: a trimmer, edger, blower, and hedge trimmer. The trimmer is used to reach grass that grows in places the mower can't reach, like around trees or mailbox posts. A commercial model will run $200 to $400. An edger removes the grass that grows over the edge of driveways, sidewalks, and other borders. A commercial motorized four-wheel model will cost around $400, while a stick edger runs about $200. A backpack blower is used to direct stray clippings back onto the lawn and can cost $200 to $550, although a commercial-quality blower may not be necessary. However, you will want to opt for one with the most powerful motor to help you get the job done faster. Finally, a hedge trimmer puts the finishing touches on those stately borders. A commercial electric model will cost

$180 to $500, but can be a pain because you have to hunt around for an outside electrical outlet. You might want to pick up a cordless rechargeable model instead, which you can get for under $100 at a home improvement store like Lowe's.

Some lawn care equipment manufacturers offer machines that are edgers and trimmers combined. Redmax makes a split-boom (shaft) multihead tool that retails for $399 that can be fitted with a $190 edger attachment. While these combination tools will save you a few bucks and some space in the garage or shed, they're not recommended for people who groom lawns for a living unless they have a very small client base—say ten customers or fewer.

tip

If you work with a partner or an employee, or if you send a crew out to a job site, a second commercial mower is a must. That way, if the person who's doing the edging, trimming, and other work finishes first, he or she can wheel out the second mower to assist the main mower.

With all the equipment you'll need, now you can see why you need a truck to operate this business!

Landscaping Necessities

The type of tools you need to start a landscaping business with depends on the type of service you plan to offer. As with a lawn service, many aspiring landscapers start with tools from their own tool shed or garage and add to the cache as the business grows. This is the preferred way to launch your business because it keeps startup costs as low as possible.

Here's a list of the basic tools you may need to work on gardens, berms, flower beds, and other areas as a landscape maintenance/gardening professional:

Digging Tools

- ▶ *Pointed and square-edged shovels*: for turning loose earth
- ▶ *Spade*: for digging up just about anything
- ▶ *Spading fork*: square-tined implement that won't bend out of shape
- ▶ *Hoe*: long-handled for cultivating; scuffle hoe for cutting weeds
- ▶ *Pick*: for piercing
- ▶ *Mattock*: for cutting and chopping roots
- ▶ *Hoses*: 50-footers are standard, with a 1-inch diameter and cast solid brass connectors
- ▶ *Dandelion tool*: a chisel-like tool that can fit in your back pocket

Cutting Tools

- ▶ *Pruners*: with a sheath
- ▶ *Loppers*: for chopping off heavy branches
- ▶ *Pruning saw*: for getting in between branches
- ▶ *Hedge shears*: the low-tech manual type for shaping topiaries, electric or gas shears for hedges
- ▶ *Commercial tool and blade sharpener*: to keep cutting edges sharp

Grading Tools

- ▶ *Lawn roller*: a heavy device (usually filled with water) that's used to level lawns
- ▶ *Hand tamper*: for compressing soil, gravel, or crushed stone
- ▶ *Power tamper (aka Jumping Jack)*: the same as a hand tamper, but gas-powered
- ▶ *Vibratory plate compactor*: for compacting soil on big jobs

Measuring Tools

- ▶ *Sighting level*: surveying instrument used to measure the angle of inclination between the user and a target
- ▶ *Tape measure*: most useful in longer lengths like 100 feet
- ▶ *Measuring wheel*: for taking onsite measurements

Marking Tools

- ▶ *Marking paint applicator*: device used to put down lines on grass, concrete, and various other surfaces
- ▶ *Chalk wheel*: for drawing temporary lines
- ▶ *Flagging tape*: for surveying, mapping, tagging, and other marking applications

Miscellaneous

- ▶ *Sledgehammer*: long-handled, two-faced hammer used to drive stakes into the ground or for other heavy pounding
- ▶ *Single jack*: a short-handled sledgehammer
- ▶ *Stake driver*: hammer for driving tree stakes
- ▶ *Basic carpenter's tools*: including hammers, hand saws, power saw, drill, level, square, plumb bob

save

There's no need to buy your own tractor for your landscaping business, even if you have enough room to store it when it's not in use. That's where it will stay most of the time because you'll rarely use it, according to experienced landscapers. Rent instead and keep your capital purchase dollars in the bank.

▶ *Leather gloves*: because gripping these tools can be murder on your hands, and because spiny weeds can cut right through regular garden gloves

▶ *Work boots*: preferably steel-toed because they give the best protection

Creature Comforts

▶ *Lip balm with SPF of at least 15*: to prevent sun damage and cracking. Try www.drugstore.com.

▶ *Gardener's hand cream*: to create a layer of protection against constant friction and weather. Concentrated, long-lasting Awakening Hands (www.awakeningskincare.com) is a gardener's favorite.

▶ *Face protectant*: to keep your face warm and protected from windburn while you're plowing those mountains of snow. Warm Skin All Weather Guard (www.warmskin.com) is the brand used by Anne Bancroft, arctic explorer.

▶ *Sunglasses*: for UVA and UVB protection, which can help prevent cataracts

▶ *Aromatherapy*: to soothe your tired body and mind at the end of a hard day. A few drops of essential oils lavender and/or clary sage on a warm, damp washcloth, draped over your face for ten minutes can do wonders. Try www.fragrancenet.com. Don't worry, we won't tell your friends you like lavender.

▶ *Seamless socks*: to prevent blisters and keep your dogs dry and comfortable. Try Wigwam IronMan Thunder Pro socks for cushioned support.

▶ *Back massager*: to motivate you to get back out there tomorrow. HoMedics (www.homedics.com) has motorized, heated seats for your truck for a great ride home.

You'll also want to wear long sleeves and goggles to protect yourself from flying debris while you're working. According to the experts, if you're buying everything new, a budget of $5,000 to $6,000 will cover the costs of your basic tools.

Basic Tools for Other Landscaping Professionals

Not every landscape career will require you to get down and dirty on the job, which means your equipment needs will be more modest. For instance, if you're planning to be an interior landscaper, basically all you'll need is a watering can, plant mister, small hand tools like

tip

Give your back a break by investing in a wheelbarrow with a hinged mechanism that allows you to tip the tub or the cart almost effortlessly. One to check out is the heavy-duty Loadumper, which has a 500-pound capacity and holds 8 cubic feet of soil or mulch. You can see it at www.homedepot.com and other sites where lawn equipment is sold.

spades and rakes for repotting or doing other small-scale maintenance, and maybe a van with your company name on the side to transport you to job sites. A gardener might need a lawn mower, rake, hoe, broom, hand tools, and a truck (or utility trailer) to transport equipment. A landscape architect or designer basically needs a computer and CAD software for designing landscapes (both of which are discussed starting on page 96.) The choice is yours—although we know how hard it can be to quell your enthusiasm for cool tools and gadgets when you get into the lawn and garden store. You might want to budget $1,000 or so to feed your flora frenzy.

Office Equipment

Though the primary equipment you'll be using in your daily business is lawn care or landscaping equipment, you can't start this business with a lawn mower and edger alone. You'll also need office equipment to keep the administrative side of your business in tip-top shape. You'll find a list of high- and low-end office equipment and supplies for two hypothetical lawn care businesses in Figure 7–3, on page 108. Then on page 109, in Figure 7–4, you can pencil in your own office equipment and supplies costs. Here's a look at the office equipment you may require to keep the business humming along.

Furniture

Since you'll be doing most of your work out in the great outdoors, you may not think it's necessary to establish a specific work space at home. After all, you can stuff invoices at the dining room table while grabbing a late-night sandwich or set up your laptop on the patio (by the fountain, of course) when you want to do your scheduling for the month, right?

Though you can run your business from whatever corner of the house that's relatively free of video games and laundry, you'll be much more productive and feel more professional if you set up a permanent office space somewhere in the house, even if it's just in a secluded corner. This is especially important if you have children around who are always clamoring for a game of catch, a ride to the park, or assistance dressing Barbie. You just need to teach them that when Daddy or Mommy is in the work space, "Sh-h-h-h-h, no interruptions!" The basic requirements for your work space are an inexpensive desk or computer workstation, a comfortable office chair (preferably one that's ergonomic, since you'll be spending a lot of time in it),

save

A sheet of sanded and stained plywood laid on top of a pair of two-drawer file cabinets makes a sturdy and inexpensive desk. The desk will be exactly the right height and will provide plenty of storage and work space.

and a sturdy two- or four-drawer file cabinet. You should also consider acquiring a bookcase so you can keep your reference materials conveniently at hand.

Office supply stores like Staples and Office Depot sell reasonably priced office furniture that will set you back only about $50 to $250 for a desk, and $50 to $200 for a chair. In addition, you often can save a substantial amount of money on your desk or computer workstation by purchasing furniture that you must assemble yourself or by scouring the classified ads for used furniture. A two-drawer letter-sized file cabinet costs $40 to $100, while a four-shelf bookcase will cost around $70 to $100.

Computers

A computer is essential to the small business; it is like having a part-time employee. You can use sophisticated yet user-friendly software packages to crunch numbers, churn out billing statements, figure your taxes, and

tip

Kelly Giard of Clean Air Lawn Care cautions against purchasing a lot of commercial equipment before you really need it. "Just buy equipment that can handle small commercial jobs and large residential ones; half an acre or less. Once your business matures and you get a big commercial account that can finance it, then go out and get that bigger ticket commercial equipment."

connect you to the internet. Best of all, the cost is reasonable, even for a fledgling small-business owner—usually around $1,000 to $1,500 for a high-speed desktop system that includes the hard drive, monitor, mouse, modem and printer, or $650 for a 64-bit laptop, which is convenient to have out in the field if you need to look something up.

Since the most common business software packages take a lot of memory, your system should have at least an 80 GB hard drive, 512 MB RAM, and a processor speed of 2.4 GHz. With inexpensive USB "thumb drives" and multiple options in "cloud" networks, storage of your records, including photos, is now relatively simple and requires little if any financial outlay.

Software

All the lawn care and landscaping business owners we spoke with use two basic software packages for conducting business: Microsoft Office and QuickBooks. QuickBooks Basic is an easy-to-use accounting package that not only keeps your financial records, but can also manage your business checking account and print checks. The basic version retails for about $200.

Microsoft Office is the most widely used office productivity software on the market. Microsoft Office Professional Edition includes Word (for word processing), Excel (for analyzing data), PowerPoint (a must for presentation materials), Access (for database management), Publisher (for creating promotional materials), and Outlook (for email). It retails for under $500. Word comes with a wide range of document templates, most of which are accessed through Microsoft's website at www.microsoft.com or Microsoft Office Online at https://products.office.com

There are also many lawn care and landscaping business software packages worth mentioning. The owners we spoke with favored CLIP from Sensible Software, Inc. (www.clip.com). Five different packages are available; installed versions of most software packages are slowly being phased out and CLIP is no exception. Subscription prices range from $50 to $80 per month depending on the features you want. Among the features they offer are scheduling, routing, and job-costing. You also can transfer billing information directly to QuickBooks to generate invoices.

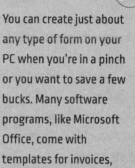

aha!

You can create just about any type of form on your PC when you're in a pinch or you want to save a few bucks. Many software programs, like Microsoft Office, come with templates for invoices, purchase orders, time sheets, and other useful forms that can be adapted to your needs.

Other green-industry-specific software programs worth checking out are Route Rite (call 818-889-1361 for price or visit www.gopst.com), with customer history, routing and consistent scheduling, accounts receivable, and inventory management functions; and GroundsKeeper Pro ($479), a comprehensive business management software package for landscapers and lawn service professionals (www.adkad.com). Marc and Lindsay of Greenwise really appreciate Real Green Service Assistant software (formerly Lawn and Pest Assistant III), which allows them to pull up routing and custom property reports on each of their clients to schedule logistics efficiently, in addition to its myriad database management features (visit www.realgreen.com). Lindsay feels that it's really geared toward helping businesses grow. See the Appendix for information on where to buy these software products.

Finally, if you're a landscaping professional, you should consider investing in a computer-aided design (CAD) program. This type of design and drafting tool not only allows you to create 3-D design layouts, but it also allows you to make any changes requested by your customers with just the click of a mouse. There are quite a number of CAD packages on the market, ranging from consumer-oriented versions, which run as little as

$39.99, to professional programs that can cost thousands of dollars. (One to consider: DynaSCAPE Design, www.dynascape.com/design/, which was tailored especially for landscape designers and costs a cool $1,995 plus $37.50 a month.) Even if you're not proficient in CAD now, you might want to invest in a package and take the training to learn how to use it. While neatly drawn landscaping plans are fine, computer-generated versions look even more professional. You'll find the names of a few companies that offer CAD software in the Appendix.

Telephones

A phone is an essential piece of equipment. If you want to maintain a landline, buy the best phone you can afford. A standard two-line speakerphone with auto redial, memory dial, flashing lights, mute button, and other useful features will run $50 to $180. A great source for professional, high-quality phones is Hello Direct, which carries the Polycom line of professional business telephones. While you're at it, consider purchasing a phone with a headset for hands-free calling so you can prevent the discomfort caused by cradling the receiver between your neck and shoulder.

aha!

Virtual offices can solve some of the problems created by working from home. Their offerings include receptionist, secretarial, and messaging services, business mailing addresses, conference rooms, part-time or full-time office availability, and even IT and marketing assistance. Visit www.regus.com and www.intelligentoffice.com to see how they work.

Your answering machine is another must-have for the times when you're away from the office or you're trying to do some paperwork without interruption. Many cordless phone units come with built-in answering machines with all the bells and whistles you need. One of the most useful features allows you to call in from a remote location and pick up your messages, which you'll appreciate when you're actively seeking new clients.

Cell phones are a given and lawn care professionals will use them to keep in touch with employees, call customers, and return calls while en route to job sites (using your hands-free built-in Bluetooth system, of course). Kelly Giard of Clean Air Lawn Care uses a Blackberry and supplies his seven youngish employees with cell phones that have both GPS and email capabilities, commenting that they will be much more likely to text him back than call him (it's a generation thing) and that the GPS has prevented many employees from getting lost on their way to important jobs.

It's important to respond to new queries immediately, especially when you consider the immediacy with which consumers shop for services; your potential customer may just call the next listing if you don't answer, rather than leave a message. Cell phones will help you not miss those jobs.

Many cellular service providers provide a brand-new phone at no charge at the time of service activation. The top five rated cell phones, according to www.pcworld.com, range in price from $150 to $879. But as important, if not more so, than the phone itself is the service you choose. Be sure you figure out which cell phone provider has the best coverage in your area of business. A cell phone is pretty useless if you aren't in range to use it. See the "Business Services" section starting on page 102 for a rundown of monthly service charges.

Copy Machines

It's not absolutely essential to have a copy machine right in your office, especially when quickie print shops like FedEx Office and Staples are so conveniently located around the country. But you can't beat the convenience of having your own copier nearby, especially now that they cost as little as $85 to $500 for a personal copier, or $1,800 and up for a stand-alone model. Camera supply warehouses such as www.bhphotovideo.com are good sources for both copiers and toner cartridges, which can also be found at your local office supply store. And you can lease instead of purchase; leases often come with built-in maintenance agreements.

A really small or part-time lawn care or landscaping business probably can do without its own copier. But if you want one, search online for the names and numbers of dealers in your area, or stop by one of the office superstores if you're looking for a smaller model.

Point-of-Sale Equipment

If you're planning to accept credit cards as a way to offer your customers the ultimate in convenience, you'll need to purchase a point-of-sale (POS) terminal, which starts at around $299, and a credit card receipt printer ($170). Be sure your credit card terminal has a chip reader, which is the direction credit cards are going across the world. Because this is desktop equipment, this setup works best for a company that does all its billing on a monthly basis from a home office. If you prefer to carry your POS equipment in your company vehicle so you can clear payments on the spot, you may find a terminal like the Hypercom T7P Standard to be more convenient, since it has a thermal printer built right in so you don't need a separate receipt printer. It runs on both AC and DC power, so when you're on the road you simply plug it into your vehicle's USB port. One last option is a wireless POS terminal. A unit like the Nurit 8000 starts at around $550 and requires a cellular phone to make it go.

It's also possible to clear credit cards using your desktop or laptop computer and a POS software package. The best thing about the software is that it costs a lot less than the POS terminal and other hardware described above. A few POS software packages you could investigate include PCCharge Pro (Verifone Systems, Inc., $249), and any of the bundled solutions offered by AccuPOS, starting at $795. Go to www.softwareadvice.com to find a list of over 200 point of sale software systems with reviews, price range, and platform information.

If you think you'll do more than $1,500 a month in sales, another option to consider is the Nutrit 8020, offered by The Credit Card Store. Their offer includes a free wireless (loaner) card terminal/printer with your merchant account, priced at 1.19 to 1.69 percent of your transaction and a $25 monthly wireless fee.

You might want to try something even simpler like the Apple POS Square card reader. It is a postage stamp-sized card that plugs into the audio input jack on your phone. It is also compatible with many devices like the iPhone, iPod Touch, iPad, Nexus One, Motorola Droid, Motorola Droid X, and more. There are no contracts or monthly fees beyond the per-card swipe rate of 2.75 percent, plus $0.15. There are many additional convenience features in Square (www.squareup.com).

Merchant Accounts

Once you have all this POS equipment, you'll need a merchant account to clear the credit card payments. A merchant account is like an electronic clearinghouse that verifies that the credit or debit card that has been presented is good. In addition to paying around $100 to establish the account, you'll pay a per-transaction fee to process sales through your POS equipment. We'll discuss merchant accounts in further detail in Chapter 13.

Office Supplies

After spending all that money on lawn care equipment, you'll be relieved to know that office supplies will cause barely a ripple in your budget. One of your most important purchases will be a box of professionally printed business cards. They don't have to be fancy. Black lettering on white card stock looks professional and gets the job done. Print shops like FedEx Office and office supply stores like Office Depot can whip up cards for you at a reasonable cost (around $15 to $50 for 1,000 business cards). There are also a number of mail-order printing companies that offer themed business cards, many with pre-designed landscape logos and layout. All you have to do is choose one that strikes your fancy and enter in your contact info. Ordering full-color business cards online starts at just $20 for 200 full-color cards at 123 Print. Between perusing a few other online printers like Amsterdam Printing

▶ Meter Matters

Though not a necessity for a small business, a postage meter is a nice time-saving device for doing large mailings. Meters can't be purchased outright (because of USPS regulations), but they can be leased for only about $20 a month for a standard model, or $20 to $120 monthly for a postage meter/electronic scale. Once you're a proud lessee, you simply load up your meter with postage online at www.usps.com, or just stop by your local post office. If you're planning to do bulk mailings, you'll also need a permit from the USPS. There is an annual cost for this renewable permit, which at the time of this writing was $220.

If you think you'll be sending out a lot of large packages (like detailed landscape drawings), you might also like to have a postage scale in your office to verify that you have sufficient postage on your parcels. A mechanical scale is very affordable at about $10 to $25. But if you think you'll be using expedited mailing services regularly, a programmable postage scale would be a smart buy at $70 to $250.

For regular first-class mail, such as invoices and other uncomplicated mail that you send regularly, you might want to look into online postage purchasing.

and NEBS (New England Business Service) and the wide variety of papers, font styles, and colors, you'll certainly find something that expresses your unique business.

Alternatively, if you're operating on a real shoestring budget, you can purchase blank business cards from an office supply store and make your own on your office printer. A pack of 250 printable business cards runs under $13 and can be produced in minutes. (This should be an emergency, last-resort measure when you run out of cards. For the most professional look, spend the extra $20 and get your cards professionally printed.)

The other thing you're going to need is invoices and No. 10 window envelopes so you can bill your clients on a regular basis. You can get 250, two-part custom-printed landscaping-business-specific invoices for $58 at www.print4less.com. While you're at it, invest in No. 10 envelopes with windows and have your company name and address imprinted on the face (500 will cost around $34). Using custom-printed invoices makes your business look professional, stable, and reliable.

Finally, you'll need estimate forms. You can make these up yourself on your printer, since the ones available in office supply stores are too general. Figure 2–1 on page 20 features a sample estimate form.

As far as other office supply costs go, you can enter $150 on the "Miscellaneous Supplies" line of the worksheet in Figure 7–4, on page 109, which will buy a lot of pens, pads, copy paper, and file folders.

Business Services

Now that you have an idea what it will cost to outfit your new business in terms of tangible goods, you also must factor in the cost of the services that are required to actually use some of those products.

Telephone charges are likely to make up the lion's share of the service fees you'll pay on a monthly basis. Useful features you'll want to consider adding to your basic service include voice mail ($15 to $20 per month), call waiting (approximately $5 to $8 per month), and caller ID (around $9 for number identification and $2 for name and number identification). However, business lines can be very costly—from $150 to as much as $400 per line, vs. $30 to $40 per month for basic residential services. For this reason, some entrepreneurs choose to install a second residential line instead, and use it exclusively for the business.

You may already have a cellular phone that you can use for business. You should know, however, that unless you use that phone for business 100 percent, you can't deduct its cost on your business taxes. You might want to think about getting a dedicated business cell phone instead, especially since they're so reasonably priced. If you have employees, you could think about getting a plan that allows for additional lines at considerable cost savings. The average price for cellular service is about $40 for 1,500 minutes and may include free in-network calling, free long distance, and rollover minutes. You can usually get a free basic phone when you activate the service, and there may be an activation fee of around $30. A smartphone with a data plan adds approximately $60 per month but also varies widely depending on what company you sign on with and how much data you think you will use in a month. It sure is handy for things like locating a parts place and finding out their hours if your equipment breaks down.

There are several internet service choices. The least expensive service is delivered by an internet service provider (ISP), which charges $20 to $25 per month for unlimited usage and uses the modem that comes with your computer. But there are many other faster internet connection options, including ISDN, DSL, and broadband. Many coffee shops offer free wifi with your morning brew, so if you've got a morning routine of stopping at one, you may consider using your tablet device to catch up on email correspondence there.

Last but not least, you may choose to rent a P.O. box or a box at a mailing center like The UPS Store as a way of keeping your business mail separate from your personal mail.

The cost of a USPS box varies widely depending on your location and the size of the box, but plan on at least $25 per month for a small box.

If you've been penciling in your estimated costs on the worksheets in Figures 7–2 and 7–4 on pages 106 and 109, respectively, as you read this chapter, you can now tally everything up to get a pretty clear idea of how much capital it will take to get your new lawn care or landscaping business started. Need a little financial help to get the ball rolling? See Chapter 13 for advice about approaching bankers and obtaining financing.

Startup Expenses

Here are the startup expenses for two hypothetical lawn care businesses that provide basic mowing and trimming services. The Yard Man is a homebased company whose owner has an office in the corner of his den. He financed the startup with his personal credit cards. The Yard Man has a projected annual gross income of approximately $36,000 a year (32 clients at $40 per week for 28 weeks of the year).

Freedom Hill Landscaping is also homebased and has top-of-the-line maintenance and business equipment. The owner employs two part-time workers at a rate of $10 per hour. It is a full-time business servicing an affluent area and expects to earn nearly $64,000 a year. It employs two people: the owner (who works full time) and one part-time helper (20 hours per week). In addition to offering landscape design, installation, and maintenance, the owner plans to offer snow plowing services during the winter to generate a steady revenue stream year-round.

Each business owner takes a percentage of the net profits as income. The Yard Man's owner uses a personal truck he already owned free and clear for the business, while Freedom Hill Landscaping's owner purchased a company vehicle as part of his startup expenses.

Item	The Yard Man	Freedom Hill Landscaping
Truck		$33,000
Locking toolbox	$200	$200
Truck dumping mechanism		$900
Trailer	$300	$1,650
Snow blade	$300	$1,000
Storage facility (6 months)		$600
Magnetic signs	$120	$120
Security system	$100	$100
Mower	$1,000	$2,500
Trimmer	$200	$400
Edger	$225	$650
Blower	$200	$200
Miscellaneous tools	$1,500	$3,000
Steel-toed boots	$90	$150
Safety equipment	$50	$50

FIGURE 7–1: **Startup Expenses Example**

Startup Expenses

Item	The Yard Man	Freedom Hill Landscaping
Shirts with company logo (5 per person)	$65	$300
Hats with company logo (1 per person)	$15	$30
Steel shelving		$50
Office equipment, furniture, supplies*	$1,800	$9,760
Employee wages (6 months)**		$4,800
Taxes/benefits (6 months)		$416
Phone (line installation charges)	$45	$45
Phone service (6 months)	$240	$240
Cell phone service (6 months)	$240	$240
Startup advertising (3% of projected revenue)	$1,100	$1,900
Legal services	$900	$900
Liability insurance (annual cost)	$300	$300
Workers' comp insurance (6 months)		$466
Market research	$200	$500
Business license	$30	$30
Pesticide applicator's license		$50
Certification/training		$250
Membership dues (annual cost)	$190	$240
Publications (annual subscriptions)	$50	$50
Online service (6 months)	$120	$240
Website design	$800	$2,500
Web hosting (6 months), domain name		$160
Merchant account (6 months)		$180
Post office box (6 months)		$120
Subtotal	$10,380	$68,287
Miscellaneous expenses (roughly 10% of subtotal)	$1,038	$6,828
Total Startup Expenses	**$11,418**	**$75,115**

*See Figure 7–3, the office equipment worksheet, on page 108 for details.

**One 20-hour-per-week employee at $10/hour

FIGURE 7–1: **Startup Expenses Example,** continued

Startup Expenses Worksheet

Item	Cost
Truck	$
Locking toolbox	$
Truck dumping mechanism	$
Trailer	$
Snow blade	$
Storage facility (6 months)	$
Magnetic signs	$
Security system	$
Mower	$
Trimmer	$
Edger	$
Blower	$
Miscellaneous tools	$
Steel-toed boots	$
Safety equipment	$
Shirts with company logo (5 per person)	$
Hats with company logo (1 per person)	$
Steel shelving	$
Office equipment, furniture, supplies	$
Employee wages (6 months)	$
Taxes/benefits (6 months)	$
Phone (line installation charges)	$
Phone service (6 months)	$

FIGURE 7–2: **Startup Expenses Worksheet**
Use this worksheet to calculate your own startup expenses.

Startup Expenses Worksheet

Item	Cost
Cell phone service (6 months)	$
Startup advertising (3% of projected revenue)	$
Legal services	$
Liability insurance (annual cost)	$
Workers' comp insurance (6 months)	$
Market research	$
Business license	$
Pesticide applicator's license	$
Certification/training	$
Membership dues (annual cost)	$
Publications (annual subscriptions)	$
Online service (6 months)	$
Website design	$
Web hosting (6 months), domain name	$
Merchant account (6 months)	$
Post office box (6 months)	$
Subtotal	$
Miscellaneous expenses (roughly 10% of subtotal)	$
Total Startup Expenses	$

FIGURE 7–2: **Startup Expenses Worksheet,** continued

Office Equipment and Supplies

Item	The Yard Man	Freedom Hill Landscaping
Office Equipment		
Computer, printer		$2,000
Intuit QuickBooks	$200	$200
Green industry software	$380	$2,500
CAD software		$1,500
Surge protector	$15	$15
Multipurpose fax/scanner/copier		$250
Copy machine		$200
Phone	$40	$100
Cell phone	$100	$100
POS equipment/software		$995
Answering machine	$25	$25
Calculator	$10	$10
Postage meter/scale	$10	$40
Digital camera		$200
Office Furniture		
Desk	$50	$250
Chair	$50	$200
File cabinet(s)	$40	$100
Bookcase(s)		$100
Office Supplies		
Stationery, invoices, business cards	$200	$200
Service brochures	$500	$500
Miscellaneous supplies (pens, folders, etc.)	$150	$150
Computer/copier paper		$25
Extra printer cartridge	$25	$25
Extra fax cartridge		$30
Extra copier toner		$15
CD-RW disks		$25
Mouse pad	$5	$5
Total	**$1,800**	**$9,760**

FIGURE 7–3: **Office Equipment and Supplies**

An example of the office equipment and supplies expenses for two fictitious businesses, The Yard Man and Freedom Hill Landscaping.

Office Equipment and Supplies Worksheet

Item	Cost
Office Equipment	
Computer, printer	$
Intuit QuickBooks	$
Green industry software	$
CAD software	$
Surge protector	$
Multipurpose fax/scanner/copier	$
Copy machine	$
Phone	$
Cell phone	$
POS equipment/software	$
Answering machine	$
Calculator	$
Postage meter/scale	$
Digital camera	$
Office Furniture	
Desk	$
Chair	$
File cabinet(s)	$
Bookcase(s)	$
Office Supplies	
Stationery, invoices, business cards	$
Service brochures	$
Miscellaneous supplies (pens, folders, etc.)	$
Computer/copier paper	$
Extra printer cartridge	$
Extra fax cartridge	$
Extra copier toner	$
CD-RW disks	$
Mouse pad	$
Total	**$**

FIGURE 7–4: **Office Equipment and Supplies Worksheet**
Use this worksheet to calculate your own office equipment and supplies startup expenses.

8

Turf
Tenders

Are you looking for a way to grow your business, unload some of the burden of its day-to-day operations, or dig your way out of a pile of paperwork? Then hire a few employees.

Lawn service and landscaping business owners usually start out as sole proprietors. But let's say you've established a nice, steady customer base that you can handle easily yourself—say, 20 regulars per week if you're mowing, or enough landscaping business to keep the bills paid each month. Then, suddenly, a really tasty piece of business drops into your lap—like the cemetery contract Ken Walkowski had in Michigan. That particular job will require you to be out mowing vast vistas and trimming between headstones all day long for a couple of weeks each month. You can't neglect your residential customers during that time or they won't be your customers for very long. So hiring an employee—or maybe two—is the answer.

Unfortunately, becoming an employer can be like opening Pandora's Box. Among the parties that will suddenly become extremely interested in you are the IRS (in addition to the keen personal interest it already has in your affairs), the Social Security Administration, OSHA, your state taxing agency, your state agriculture department (if you handle chemicals), and so on. It's enough to make a grown business owner cry. The trick is to do your crying all the way to the bank. So in this chapter, we'll show you some efficient ways to hire, motivate, and compensate in the pursuit of bigger profits.

Diving into the Labor Pool

Finding qualified help can be a real challenge. While mowing or planting doesn't necessarily take a great deal of technical skill, it is hard work, and often done under uncomfortably warm conditions. It also takes a fair amount of physical stamina and the ability to handle power tools deftly without amputating useful body parts. So what on earth would make someone take on such a demanding job when he or she could sell designer shoes at the mall or call out mystery game numbers at the bowling alley?

M-O-N-E-Y, that's what. Which is why you'll have to do better than minimum wage if you want to attract qualified workers.

Three of the landscape professionals we talked to pay their employees above the national average, but they also have high expectations for output. Nathan Bowers in Sykesville, Maryland, keeps his employees a long time with that strategy. Kelly Giard in Colorado pays his workers a percentage of each sale they make, and that keeps them motivated to always promote the company. He says that works out well for both parties. Remember that the trade-off for shelling out the big bucks is that, like Bowers, you won't have to spend a lot of time advertising, interviewing, and hiring if you keep those good employees. But you don't necessarily have to break the bank to get the same excellent results. The Bureau of Labor Statistics reports that the current estimated median hourly wage for landscaping and groundskeeping laborers was $12.03. If that's a little too high for your startup budget, you could instead offer at least $2 above minimum wage since it's hard to find unskilled jobs that pay that well.

However, according to industry experts and other business owners we spoke to, $11 to $14 an hour is about the going hourly rate for employees, which, compared to the current minimum wage, looks pretty darned good. Some owners, like Steve Mager, a lawn care business owner in Minnesota who also does chemical applications, have a sliding wage scale. Steve's base wage is $10, but he pays more—around $15 an hour—to workers with certain qualifications, such as those with a spotless driving record or a pesticide certification.

When you establish your base wage, keep in mind that in service industries like lawn care, it's not unusual for workers to change jobs to nab as little as a 25-cent-per-hour pay increase. It's a good idea to ask around to see what other service providers are paying in your area and set your base pay rate accordingly.

Good Company Culture

Higher pay isn't necessarily the most powerful tool for attracting and keeping good employees. Other perks like gifts and empowering treatment by the boss can create long-time loyalty the same way a little extra money can.

Assuming you're starting with carefully chosen employees, you can nurture growth in each employee and help them achieve career and educational goals while on the job. Tuition reimbursement can be expensive, but if you hire a professional trainer to educate and certify your employees in groups, it can be much more cost effective. Enriching your company and your employees' credentials at the same time inspires confidence in both parties. Employees feel valued by your investment in them and they get skills they can use for a lifetime. You can set goals for incremental pay raises earned by their participation in a certain number of classes.

Plant identification, proper handling and cleaning of tools (like chainsaws, chippers, and snowblowers), xeriscaping, native plant selection, and irrigation installation are examples of training advancement. There are a number of freebies out there, too, such as the Water Smart Landscape Program Certification offered by the Municipal Water District of Orange County (www. ocwatersmart.com/landscape). Check your area for free training programs like this one.

Other ways to inspire your team may be with free movie or sporting event tickets or a bimonthly massage certificate for those aching backs and arms. Massage

aha!

Schools and universities that have agriculture, landscape, or horticulture departments can be great sources of prospective employees. Not only are these students more likely to be interested in working in the field, but they'll also come to you with more knowledge about horticulture than the average person.

Envy (www.massageenvy.com), a franchise of massage therapy clinics in 49 states, offers group and corporate rates and massages at a reasonable cost for 50 glorious minutes.

Creativity, teamwork, and perfect attendance should be acknowledged, if not rewarded in some way. A great manager can get so much more out of his/her workers than one who is not engaged or who only cares about the bottom line. If you pour your energy into the right people, they will usually reward you with extra effort, more pride in workmanship, and initiative on the job.

The Chase Begins

Unless you have a few unemployed family members or neighbors positively panting for the chance to unleash your powerful beast of a mower on an unsuspecting lawn, you're going to have to do a little work to find qualified help. Even in this day and age of online job searching, the classified ads of your local paper are still the logical starting place for launching an employee search. The cost to advertise is usually fairly low, and you often can get a break on the price of the ad by running it several times. Make no mistake about it—you will have to run your ad more than once to smoke out the best candidates. Luckily, you don't need highly trained workers, but you do need reliable people who are willing to work hard. Having a bigger pool of candidates to draw from will allow you to choose more carefully.

tip

Social media networking is an excellent tool for getting to know prospective job candidates. Sites such as Facebook and LinkedIn are where you can see an overview of personalities by viewing profiles. LinkedIn is the most professional of the sites and where you'll find mature candidates with higher education and specialized skills, such as landscape design. Facebook is the social networking site with the most members. Users display a mix of professional and social pages, and word searches such as "landscaper" and "student" will help you find them.

Because you'll be competing with gas stations, pizzerias, and other small businesses for the same crop of employees, you might want to bypass the line ads, which are those little three- to five-line ads that look like a black blur when you open up the paper and glance at the page, and instead take out a display ad. Display ads are the larger, boxed ads, which automatically stand out from the rest. Often, they also include elements like artwork and bold type and may even have color, depending on the newspaper's capabilities. They cost more than line ads, of course, but they can be worth the price, and you usually can work a deal with the paper's advertising sales department to get a discounted multiple insertion rate. Some lawn and landscaping business owners even run their ads continuously throughout the green season.

Now that the 21st century is in full swing, you can't overlook the power and reach of web-based job boards like www.indeed.com, www.idealist.org, and www.monster.com or your local newspaper's own internet classified section when you're looking for help. Even Craig's List (www.craigslist.org) has become a go-to place for job seekers. They're usually quite affordable, and you really can leave your ad out there in cyberspace indefinitely if you wish. Just don't forget to indicate exactly where the job is located, especially when using national job boards.

Ready to try your hand at advertising? Here are a couple of sample display ads:

Residential Lawn Care Worker

Part-time position for enthusiastic, reliable person who can handle large commercial lawn mower. No experience necessary—will train the right person. Competitive wages. Send letter of interest to:

Buzz Cuts

1142 Grandy Ave., Munger, OR 97010

Landscaping Crew Chief Wanted

Full-time job for an experienced landscaper who can direct a small crew. Duties include planning and scheduling jobs, supervising labor, and taking the lead on installation work. Competitive wages. Email resume to Freedom Hill Landscaping, info@freedomhilllandscaping.com, or fax to (555) 555-000. No phone calls, please.

The people who are most likely to respond to your ad will be young, inexperienced, possibly uneducated, and possibly nonnative speaking. But that's not necessarily a bad thing. Assuming your laborers are cooperative and eager to work (something you'll have to determine during an interview), you can teach them the right way (translation: your way) to do the job and turn them into real pros.

Nathan Bowers and the Greenwise team of Lindsay Stame and Marc Wise have the most luck finding qualified employees through word of mouth. Marc Wise feels that even though he uses basic outlets like Craigslist, the more technical and skilled job openings, like those of designers, call for referrals.

Back to School

Because so many kids today still do cut lawns or shovel snow after school to make a little green stuff, you might also want to turn them loose on your green stuff—e.g., offer them a job as a lawn or landscape maintenance helper. The local high school or even a community college can be a fertile source of job prospects, and you have the added benefit of being able to attract some of the area's strongest young people who should be able to handle power equipment. Check with your local secondary school system to find out if you can participate in its job fair or career day activities, which are held so students can meet with business owners and other professionals from a wide array of industries and companies to get them thinking about a future career. Just make sure you clear your employee search intentions with the school's principal first. Alternatively, you can ask whether the high schools have a work release program for vocational studies students who are not planning to attend college. These kids could end up being strong job candidates for your company.

tip

In certain parts of the country, nonnative speakers make up a big part of the minimum wage worker pool. If you need help communicating with your Hispanic laborers, for example, try logging on to www. freetranslation.com or www.babelfish.com, where you can type in an English phrase or sentence and have it translated for you. Keep sentences as simple as possible for the most accurate translation.

If you do meet students during one of these school-sponsored events who are at least 18 and are interested in a job, take down their contact information and arrange to have them come in for an interview right away. (Avoid hiring anyone under 18, because even though they may work legally in many parts of the country, they may not have the upper-body strength needed to handle power tools safely.) If you don't want to invite candidates into your home office, arrange to meet at an agreed-upon public location, like a coffee shop, where you can buy them a latte, have them fill out a job application, and gauge their maturity and responsibility level.

Other locations where you may be able to unearth qualified help of any age include any place you go where you personally get exceptional service, like at the gas station, a convenience store, or a restaurant; the professional organizations you belong to (other members may have college-age kids with time on their hands who need extra money); the local landscape or horticulture school or organization; and the local unemployment office, which may operate a job bank at no charge to you and the applicants.

Giving 'Em the Third Degree

Once you've identified a few promising prospects, you'll have to sit down with each one and determine his or her suitability for the job. Before the interview, have the candidate fill out a job application form, then refer to it as you ask questions. (We've also provided a list of possible questions in Figure 8–1 you can use.) But don't just talk—listen carefully to the person planted in front of you. You'll want to hire people who are enthusiastic, friendly, and articulate, as well as those with a strong work ethic. Experience is great, too—but don't pass up a good candidate just because he or she doesn't have on-the-job experience. Neophytes who receive good training can turn into good, cooperative, loyal employees.

You also should ask each candidate for a list of references, preferably compiled before the interview. Check these references carefully, because employees have been known to exaggerate on employment applications. In some cases, this can lead to disastrous results. (Imagine blithely trusting someone who claims to have hands-on experience with

---

Possible Interview Questions

▶ Where did you/do you go to school?

▶ What's your favorite subject? Why?

▶ When did you graduate?

▶ What kinds of work have you done?

▶ What would your last boss say about the work you did?

▶ Have you ever mowed lawns before (or trimmed bushes, planted flowers, etc.)?

▶ Why do you want to be a lawn or landscaping technician?

▶ Are you good with people? What makes you think so?

▶ What would you do if a client wasn't satisfied with the job you were doing?

▶ Do you have any references? May I call them?

FIGURE 8–1: **Possible Interview Questions**
Arm yourself with this list of questions when checking out employee candidates.

herbicides to service your commercial accounts, then finding out he was prevaricating when he fries your best customer's award-winning landscaping.)

Even when you do everything right, it's still possible to pick the wrong candidate—and not figure that out until after the person has been hired. Minnesota lawn care business owner Steve Mager found that out the hard way when a new hire "turned out to be a nightmare," he says. "He crashed the snow plow into a building and a car and stole $500 in fuel from me. Because of that experience, I haven't hired anyone in a while."

It's not always possible to see through a person's outward appearance to the irresponsible guy or gal underneath. You might want to have a 90-day probationary period as a condition of continued employment. Otherwise, if you fire someone, you may find yourself shelling out unemployment money to someone who's incompetent or just not the right match. Illinois landscaper Marc Wise warns potential employees that work is very hard when he hires them on the condition of a 30-day probationary period. He figures that if they can make it through 30 days and do well, that that's enough time for both parties to evaluate the situation. He adds that a bad hire brings the whole company down. "When someone's not the right fit, you're not the right fit for them either. Take care of it as soon as possible and don't avoid the confrontation. It's what's best for the other employees."

Don't forget that both U.S. citizens and noncitizens must fill out Form I-9, Employment Eligibility Verification, and present documents verifying their eligibility to work in this country before they can begin a new job. The employer must retain this form in the employee's personnel file for three years after the date of hire or one year after termination, whichever is later.

warning

Because Kelly Giard's Clean Air Lawn Care is also a franchise, he gets to learn from not only his own mistakes, but also all of his franchisees. One of them in Seattle sent a worker to a client's home to prune some blackberry bushes. He made a mistake and destroyed her 50-year-old Japanese maple tree. Kelly still remembers the shrieking customer on the phone. He bought and planted another maple, and it all turned out fine in the end. The moral of the story is to know thy plants and keep employees educated!

Making a Good Impression

Even though lawn and landscaping work can be down and dirty, it's still important for your employees to make a good impression on clients (and their neighbors), especially since their appearance is a reflection on your company. It's a good idea to establish a dress code, which might include collared shirts with your logo on them (no Marilyn Manson T-shirts on your watch!), pants, jeans, or shorts that fit and don't have holes, and appropriate footwear (steel-toed boots are recommended for safety's sake when working with power equipment). Plus, you should always insist that the men keep their shirts on, even when the sun has been turned up to "broil." The opposite sex might find the sight of bare-chested young hunks entertaining, but it just doesn't look professional, which is what you must be if you want to be taken seriously as a business owner.

To increase the likelihood that both you and your workers always look presentable, consider investing in company shirts that have your name stitched on the pocket. Colorado landscaper Kelly Giard kept his stockbroker job for a while when he first started Clean Air Lawn Care. He was called out to a job by an employee to fix a lawn mower and remembers suddenly realizing how ridiculous he looked, yanking on the starter in 100-degree weather in his Italian business suit. As discussed earlier, monogrammed shirts are very affordable and really ratchet up the professionalism of your company. It's a good idea to send workers out to job sites with spare shirts in the truck just in case they have a hard day and end up wearing more lawn and dirt than they tend.

Many lawn and landscaping business owners also enforce personal appearance standards for their employees. Despite the nature of the work, it's not too much to ask employees to be well-groomed when they arrive at a jobsite. Facial hair and long hair are OK as long as both are neat and clean; long hair on a person of either sex should be pulled back and secured to keep it from getting devoured by a roaring piece of power equipment. Body piercings and tattoos are acceptable in this day and age—as long as they're not offensive. If a worker has body art, make it a condition of employment that it must be kept covered during working hours.

Giving the Taxman His Due

Naturally, when it comes to employees, paychecks, and bonuses, you won't be able to escape the notice of one very interested party in Washington—namely, your dear old Uncle Sam.

stat fact

The Washington-based Tax Foundation, a nonpartisan educational organization, says that approximately 138.3 million tax returns were filed in 2013, the latest year for which records are available, which is 2.2 million more than in 2012. "The top 1 percent," the findings show, "of taxpayers paid a higher effective income tax than any other group, at 27.1 percent, which is over 8 times higher than taxpayers in the bottom 50 percent."

He'll be watching you closely to make sure you fork over enough taxes—both from your own pocket and from employee withholding—to meet federal guidelines. As an employer, you must withhold the following taxes from each employee's pay:

▶ Income tax
▶ FICA (aka Social Security)
▶ Medicare

You're also required to keep careful records of this withholding and send the cash off to the government at regular intervals (usually quarterly). Your accountant can be a big help in making sure you withhold and send in enough money on time. For more information about withholding and taxes, pick up a copy of IRS Publication 15, *Employer's Tax Guide*, as well as Publication 583, *Starting a Business and Keeping Records*. Both are available online at www.irs.gov or at your local IRS office.

But wait, there's more! As the owner of a business, you must pay (and you might want to sit down for this):

▶ The matching portion of each employee's FICA withholding
▶ The matching portion of Medicare taxes
▶ Federal Unemployment Tax (FUTA), which pays for unemployment insurance programs
▶ State unemployment tax
▶ Self-employment tax (that's the Social Security tax you pay on your personal earnings for the privilege of having your own business)
▶ Workers' compensation insurance (covers the medical expenses and disability benefits for employees injured on the job); your state labor department will be happy to tell you how much to send in.

If you ever wondered why people are tempted to risk the wrath of the IRS and pay their employees (or themselves) under the table, you now know why. But trust us: It's not worth it. By not reporting income (yours or your employees'), you jeopardize your ability to buy a home or car, take out loans to put your kids (or yourself) through college, and/or undertake any other legal transaction that requires credit checks and income verification. (After all, if you're not on the books, you have no income to show.)

Evading taxes is unethical and can leave you in a world of hurt if that uncle we mentioned earlier ever catches on. Think he's too busy to worry about a fledgling little lawn or landscaping business in Anytown, USA? Think again. All it takes is one vengeful ex-spouse, one unhappy customer, or one disgruntled employee with a phone or a computer to turn you in. You won't just get a slap on the hand and a fine. We're talking jail time here—five years for each count of tax evasion, plus penalties and court costs. No doubt we speak for business owners everywhere when we say nothing is worth all that hassle.

Some people try to hedge their bets with the IRS by "employing" independent contractors rather than hiring people the old-fashioned way. In theory, that sounds like a great deal. Independent contractors are not actually employed by your company, but do work for you. For a lawn or landscaping company, that could be anything from answering phones and keeping the books to trimming bushes and applying fertilizer. The problem is, if that person works the hours you set and/or uses the tools you provide, or works in your office (e.g., in a clerical capacity), the IRS views that person as an employee rather than a contractor, and as such is subject to the bushels of taxes we mentioned earlier. In fact, here's exactly what the IRS has to say about employees: "A general rule is that anyone who performs services for you is your employee if you can control what will be done and how it will be done."

That pretty much sums up the employer/employee relationship you'll be establishing with all the folks who work for you. So if you want to err on the side of caution (recommended), put all your workers on the payroll. For more information about the employee/contractor distinction, visit the IRS' website at www.irs.gov, and download Publication 15-A, *Employers' Supplemental Tax Guide*, or pick up a copy from your nearest IRS field office. Also, take a look at the "Employee or Contractor?" chart, Figure 8–2, on page 122.

stat fact

A U.S. National Health and Nutrition Examination Survey conducted by Dr. Wen Qi Gan, from the School of Environmental Health at the University of British Columbia, between 1999 and 2004 linked constant exposure to loud industrial noise and heart disease. It revealed that the workers exposed to such noise were three or four times more likely to experience angina, coronary artery disease, or heart attack and had higher-than-normal diastolic blood pressure. Hearing loss isn't the only reason to wear ear muffs.

Promoting Workplace Safety

When it comes to the possibility of being injured on the job, lawn and landscaping work ranks with some of the most dangerous occupations around. OK, so maybe green work isn't right up there with, say, snake handling or high-rise window washing, but you'll be handling sharp instruments of all kinds, spraying potentially hazardous chemicals, and using noisy equipment, all of which have the potential to cause serious injury. For these reasons, your

Employee or Contractor?

The IRS has strict guidelines and interpretations about the distinction between employees and independent contractors. The agency has developed the following 20-factor test to help determine whether a person is an independent contractor or an employee in disguise.

Factor	Employee	Independent Contractor
Instructions	Complies with instructions	Sets own rules regarding when, where, and how he/she works
Training	Receives from employer	Obtains independently
Integration	Services are important to daily operations	Business can operate without his/her services
Services	Completes work personally	Can hire others to do the work
Assistants	Doesn't hire, supervise, or pay assistants	Can hire own assistants
Relationship	Works on regular or recurring basis	Doesn't have continuing relationship
Schedule	Works hours set by employer	Works own hours
Hours worked	Works full time for one employer	Works for many employers
Location	Works on company premises	Doesn't have to work on premises
Work sequence	Follows instructions, routines	Doesn't follow set sequence
Reports	Accountable to employer for daily activities	Not accountable for daily tasks
Payment	Paid by hour, week, or month	Paid by the job
Expenses	Paid for by employer	Pays own overhead expenses
Tools	Furnished by employer	Furnishes own materials
Investment	Has no investment in tools, facility used	Has significant investment in tools, facility used
Profit or loss	Not subject to losses	Makes profit or suffers loss
Number of employers	Works for one at a time	May work for many at a time
Service availability	Not available to others for work	Can work for multiple companies
Right to fire	Can be fired at any time	Must be paid under terms of contract
Right to quit	Can quit at any time	Must meet contract terms

FIGURE 8–2: **Employee or Contractor?**

work will be governed by the standards of the Occupational Safety and Health Act of 1970. These standards deal with everything from protecting your workers from injury when using hazardous chemicals (e.g., anything that can be inhaled, including, but not limited to, fertilizer and lawn chemicals) to protecting them against noise-induced hearing loss. For more information on OSHA regulations and your responsibilities as an employer, refer to OSHA's website at www.osha.gov. In the meantime, be sure to make basic safety equipment like hearing protectors and goggles standard issue for yourself and your employees when you're working with power tools and other equipment.

Call in the Reinforcements

If all these costs, regulations, and restrictions are making you reconsider this hiring thing, don't despair. If you're so inclined, you can turn over all the administrative details to a professional employer organization (PEO), a type of company that handles all the paperwork and other administrative functions. PEOs form a legal partnership with the business owner to handle his or her company's nonproductive employee administration activities, including human resources, payroll, government regulation compliance, taxes, and record keeping. In essence, the PEO becomes the employer of record and "leases" the employee back to the business. The trade-off is that the lawn service or landscaping business owner can then turn his or her attention solely to running and marketing the business.

> **tip** (i)
>
> The Zenith (www.thezenith.com), a workers' compensation and safety education provider, advises wearing a face shield when using trimmers, brush cutters, and chippers, and a hardhat while trimming trees.

For tax reporting purposes, the business's employees fall under the PEO's federal tax ID and are recognized as its employees. PEOs often offer Fortune 500 benefits like 401(k) plans and cafeteria-style health insurance, thanks to the economies of scale a pool of hundreds or even thousands of workers can bring.

Many PEOs will handle companies with as few as two or three employees at a cost that typically runs between 1.5 and 9 percent of the company's gross payroll. While that may sound steep, it can be a good bargain for owners who would rather have a root canal than deal with paperwork and government regulations.

Planting
the Seeds
of Success

Just when you thought it was safe to go back in the water, BAM! The jaws of uncertainty open wide the moment you're faced with a unique situation or a problem you aren't sure how to handle. Maybe you're called on to repair the unsightly damage caused by overfertilization (caused by the homeowner's ex-lawn service provider, of course). Or you're unable to get a crucial part for your favorite mower (or edger or other power tool) in time to service your elaborate (and lucrative) country club account. Or maybe you've just run into a rough patch when it comes to collections and aren't comfortable strong-arming your clients.

This is where the professional development opportunities and information available through professional associations, industry publications, and university courses can be very helpful. These valuable resources can help you expand your general knowledge, spark new thinking and ideas, and keep you informed about industry developments. They're also valuable as a way to introduce you to "real world" situations and challenges. Finally, associations have an added benefit: They often permit you to use their official logo and name on your business cards, which is a signal to potential customers that you're a professional who takes your business seriously.

Here's a look at some of these professional resources. You'll find contact information for everything listed here, plus much more, in the Appendix.

Industry Associations

Lawn care and landscaping industry associations can be some of your best resources in this business. Here are a few you might want to investigate.

AmericanHort

Created from a consolidation of the American Nursery & Landscape Association and OFA—the Association of Horticultural Professionals, AmericanHort counts those who grow, distribute, and retail plants of all types, plus those who design and install landscapes for residential and commercial customers, among its membership. It provides education, research, public relations, and representation services to members, as well as legislative action and compliance information, discounted business-building publications, insurance programs, credit card processing, and rental car discounts, among other benefits. Visit http://americanhort.org/ for more information.

Association of Professional Landscape Designers

Formed in 1989, the Association of Professional Landscape Designers (APLD) promotes and supports the highly qualified professional landscape designer. It offers a certification program (discussed on page 133) and benefits such as continuing education; regulatory assistance; complimentary subscriptions to its publication, *The Designer*, and several other

green industry publications; an international directory; and a speakers bureau. In addition, APLD's website (www.apld.org) offers extensive resources for members, nonmembers, professionals, and consumers, including listings of nursery, landscape, and design associations, a database of the universities that offer green industry courses and degrees, plant information, order forms, a consumer brochure you can use to market your business (available for a fee), and much more. This is a worthwhile resource even if you aren't ready to join. Professional membership status is $290, plus the additional region-specific chapter dues ranging from $30 to $80 and filing fees.

National Gardening Association

While this organization is meant for the general public, you can still learn a lot from the National Gardening Association (NGA). Founded in 1973, the NGA is a leader in plant-based education, providing various materials (including free newsletters) that are meant to cultivate an appreciation of gardening as a hobby. The nonprofit's website also is a cornucopia of useful information. For more information check their website at www.garden.org.

National Association of Landscape Professionals

The National Association of Landscape Professionals (formerly PLANET, Professional Landcare Network) serves lawn care professionals, exterior maintenance contractors, installation/design/building professionals, and interiorscapers. The national organization was founded in 2005 with the merger of two longtime green industry organizations: the Professional Lawn Care Association of America (organized in 1979) and the Associated Landscape Contractors of America (founded in 1961). The new organization has an educational foundation, facilitates peer-to-peer sharing, and provides members with access to the best ideas and practices in the landscape industry. They also offer a comprehensive certification program (discussed on page 133) and more. Membership for green industry service providers is $350 for companies with revenues under $200,000 and $595 for companies with revenues of $200,000 to $750,000. Find them at www.landscapeprofessionals.com.

Industry Publications

A good way to stay current on news, information, events, and trends in the lawn care and landscaping industries is by subscribing to publications that serve both the owner and the consumer. Here's a brief rundown of some of the best-known publications that can keep you plugged into this industry.

Trade Publications

Grounds Maintenance

Published by Penton Media, *Grounds Maintenance* is a free, online magazine, which provides in-depth technical information for golf and green industry professionals. See http://grounds-mag.com.

aha!

Annual trade shows and conventions are great places to network and gain knowledge. Besides workshops and seminars, they often have a trade show area where vendors and suppliers to the green industry ply their wares and services, allowing you to get up close and personal with the best and brightest in the business.

Landscape Management

This free monthly magazine provides a wealth of information to people in the green industry, including those involved in landscape management, athletic turf, "golfdom," and turfgrass in general. Questex Media folded it's newsletter Turfgrass Trends into its newsletter Golfdom (www.golfdom.com) so look for the latest turfgrass information there.. In addition, the magazine's main website (http://landscapemanagement.net) provides extensive links to information on industry associations, disease management, turfgrass management, university programs, and current weather.

Lawn & Landscape

This monthly publication is the premier source for timely turfgrass news and information. Each issue tackles topics like residential mowing prices, proper pesticide application, add-on services that increase profits, and tips for sports field maintenance. It's offered free to landscape contractors, lawn maintenance and chemical lawn care companies, landscape architects, and others who provide green industry services. Published by GIE Media, Inc. Visit www.lawnandlandscape.com for more information.

ProGardenBiz Landscape & Garden Magazine

An ezine loaded with basic tips, industry insight, and more, a recent issue of *ProGardenBiz Landscape & Garden* magazine discussed how to start and run a landscape business, a piece on gophers, computer aided design (CAD), herb gardening, and mow and edging tips. The magazine is free, but the publishers make a humble request for a small donation for your subscription—and it's worth it. Sign up at www.progardenbiz.com. This website is a gem—it's loaded with industry insight and tips, and has a web portal with a discussion board and other useful interactive features. You'll also find free templates and forms. Published by ProGardenBiz.

Green Industry Pros Magazine

Known as the business management resource for landscaping professionals, this national trade magazine provides landscape professionals with timely business information. Its focus is on productivity, trends, and innovative techniques. Qualified lawn and landscape contractors can subscribe for free. The magazine also offers a free enewsletter through its website (www.greenindustrypros.com). Published seven times a year by SouthComm Business Media.

Sports Turf Manager

This quarterly magazine is a free perk if you are a member of Sports Turf Managers Association (STMA), an Ontario association dedicated to providing turf management education and resources to its members. You may also subscribe without membership for a fee. Membership is open to anyone with an interest in the sports turf industry. Topics speak to professionals working with municipal parks, schools, community colleges, universities, professional sports clubs, golf superintendents, landscape architects, landscape contractors, and sod producers. See http://sportsturfonline.com.

Turf Magazine

This magazine is written for professional landscape and mowing contractors, lawn care companies, chemical applicators, irrigation contractors, and landscape architects. Qualified business owners can receive the monthly publication free of charge. Published by Grand View Media. See www.turfmagazine.com.

fun fact ☺

The primary purposes of turfgrass management are soil stabilization, water conservation, and the filtration of air- and water-borne pollutants, according to the Texas A&M University College of Agriculture and Life Sciences. Actively growing turf also controls environmental pollution like dust, glare, and noise, and dissipates heat, especially in the country's most arid regions.

Consumer Publications

Better Homes and Gardens

Possibly the best-known of the home and garden publications, this monthly magazine was founded in 1922 and boasts a readership of over 7 billion. It has several major garden features in every issue. Published by Meredith Corp., *BHG* offers specials on annual subscription rates ranging from $6 to $11. See www.bhg.com.

Mother Earth News

Mother Earth News is one of the most popular and longest running organic gardening and sustainable lifestyle magazines, focusing on bringing readers closer to nature, sustainable farming, modern homesteading, nature and community, and renewable energy. A one-year subscription is $17. It is published by Ogden Publications, Inc. See www.motherearthnews.com.

University Courses

Quite a few universities across the United States have full-fledged turfgrass science programs that culminate in a Bachelor of Science degree. They're almost always offered through the schools' college of agriculture, so you're not likely to find such programs in urban schools. Some of these universities, like Ohio State and Penn State, also offer continuing education and "short courses" for lawn care professionals who wish to augment their knowledge of agriculture in general and turfgrass in particular without entering a formal degree program. Check with the school's agriculture department for information on these courses.

We've provided contact information for a number of universities that offer turfgrass management courses in the Appendix. For an extensive listing of programs and courses in landscape design, check out the Association of Professional Landscape Designers website at https://www.apld.org.

Colorado landscaper and franchiser Kelly Giard feels that the most important continuing education he's gotten since starting his business is that regarding search engine optimization. Learning how web-based marketing works has made a huge difference in the business he gets and how he sets up estimates for his franchise owners. Understanding how web traffic and Google searches call up different websites has created cost-effective differences in how he uses his own website. Subjects like irrigation, outdoor lighting, soil chemistry, and turfgrass management will season your maturity as a knowledgeable,

▶ Green Degrees

Many universities in the United States offer programs in turfgrass management, landscape architecture, and other related fields. Some of these university programs can be found at:

▶ *Auburn University*: Turfgrass Management (College of Agriculture)

▶ *Clemson University*: Turfgrass Management and the Ornamental Program (College of Agriculture, Forestry and Life Sciences); Landscape Architecture (College of Architecture, Arts and Humanities)

▶ *Columbia University*: Landscape Design (Masters of Science, School of Professional Studies)

▶ *Cornell University*: Soil and Crop Sciences Section (School of Integrative Plant Science)

▶ *Michigan State University*: Crop and Soil Sciences (College of Agriculture and Natural Resources); Landscape Architecture (School of Planning, Design and Construction)

▶ *Ohio State University*: Turfgrass Science (Department of Horticulture and Crop Science)

▶ *Penn State University*: Center for Turfgrass Science (College of Agricultural Sciences)

▶ *Texas A&M University*: Agronomy and Plant and Soil Science (College of Agriculture and Life Sciences)

▶ *University of California, Berkeley*: Department of Landscape Architecture and Environmental Planning (College of Environmental Design)

▶ *University of Colorado*: Turf Management (College of Agricultural Sciences)

▶ *University of Florida*: Turfgrass Science (Institute of Food and Agricultural Sciences); Landscape Architecture (Department of Landscape Architecture)

▶ *University of Georgia*: Crop and Soil Science (College of Agricultural and Environmental Sciences)

▶ *University of Illinois at Urbana-Champagne*: Bachelor of Landscape Architecture or Master of Landscape Architecture (Department of Landscape Architecture)

▶ *University of Kentucky*: Plant and Soil Science (College of Agriculture, Food, and Environment)

You can find an extensive listing with additional turfgrass management degree programs on the Landscape Management website at http://landscapemanagement.net (click on "Links" at the bottom of the homepage which takes you to an Industry Links page).

versatile service provider, but don't forget about courses that will bring your skills to the masses.

Online Resources

Got a problem that has you stumped? On the internet, you'll find a plethora of green industry online resources that can help. In addition to the wealth of knowledge available from associations and universities like the ones listed in this chapter, there are many websites, bulletin boards, and chat rooms you can log onto to get answers to your thorniest questions.

warning

In addition to the mandatory licensing required nationwide for pesticide application, the use of a respirator and gloves, along with proper care and handling of materials, is also encouraged. OSHA offers a respirator guide online to ensure proper selection, use of, and maintenance for your respirator to keep you safe. See www. osha.gov/SLTC/etools/ respiratory/respirator_ selection.html.

- ▶ *APLD*: https://www.apld.org (extensive green industry resources)
- ▶ *Cyberlawn*: http://opei.org (offers a guide to power equipment and links to other lawn and garden information; sponsored by the Outdoor Power Equipment Institute)
- ▶ *GardenWeb*: www.gardenweb.com (online forum for gardening enthusiasts)
- ▶ *Grounds Maintenance*: www.grounds-mag.com (various industry resources, as well as links to the periodical's articles and an enewsletter, *Maintenance Matters*)
- ▶ *Landscape Management*: www.landscapemanagement.net (LM blog and links to national and international associations, and information on diseases, environmental issues, general turfgrass issues, and more. It also has a listing of university programs in turfgrass management.)
- ▶ *Lawn & Landscape magazine*: www.lawnandlandscape.com (virtual trade show, bulletin board, business forms, and other resources; available only to qualified subscribers)
- ▶ *Lawnservicing.com*: www.lawnservicing.com (lawn care service business information resources, including the GrassMasters lawn service message forum and extensive links to industry resources)
- ▶ *Lawnsite.com*: www.lawnsite.com (message board for commercial lawn, landscaping, and snow plowing discussions)

You'll find additional resources in the Appendix under "Green Industry Websites."

Certification

The following organizations offer various certifications relevant to lawn care and landscaping professionals.

Association of Professional Landscape Designers

The APLD offers a national certification program that measures knowledge of design elements. You must be an APLD associate member in good standing and have a minimum of two years of landscape design experience to become certified. Other requirements include a minimum of 12 credit hours in landscape design courses and successful completion of the certification examination.

> **tip** ⓘ
>
> Earning a certification through an industry association demonstrates to your customers that you take your business seriously and are up-to-date on the latest techniques and technologies the industry has to offer.

Members are then permitted to use the APLD designation after their name. The APLD does not offer an educational curriculum and instead recommends that courses be taken at accredited educational institutions such as universities, or at botanical gardens.

Recertification is required every three years and requires 30 continuing education unit contact hours, which can be earned though participation in any green industry event (including industry conferences, seminars, and classes).

National Association of Landscape Professionals

Formerly known as PLANET, the National Association of Landscape Professionals' (NALP) Landscape Certification Programs offer seven different levels of certifications. The programs are self-study; materials are purchased through the NALP bookstore. The Lawn Care Manager test requires testing within one year of registering; for all others you have three years. Every two years you need to recertify by reporting continuing education to them that totals 24 continuing education units.

Spreading the Word

I n the musical *Hello Dolly!* Dolly Levi exclaims, "Money—pardon my expression—is like manure. It's not worth a thing unless it's spread around encouraging young things to grow." That also essentially sums up the theory behind advertising.

Basically, you have to spend money to make money. Businesses advertise regularly because they want to reach their audience as quickly as possible to showcase new products, tout innovative services, and establish a corporate image. Small businesses advertise because their livelihood and longevity depend on it.

This chapter examines a number of advertising techniques that can be used to make your business the familiar choice for customers who are seeking a quality lawn care or landscaping company.

► Bigger Fish to Fry

Once you've been in business for a while and feel you can easily handle the rigors of running the show on all fronts, it might be time to expand—either by taking on more residential customers or by dipping your toe into the waters of commercial business. If you go for the latter, you'll need to refine your marketing efforts somewhat since marketing to businesses requires a more sophisticated approach.

Focus your sales efforts on office complexes, churches, municipal parks, and other public areas by sending a brief business letter to them (each one personalized using a word processing mail merge program). Remind them of the value of well-kept grounds in terms of corporate image and property value, then point out how an outside lawn or landscaping service is much more cost-effective than having a person on staff. Also emphasize the features that make your service unique (and better than the competition) in case they use an outside service but are considering switching. Then after a week or so, make a follow-up call to request an appointment with the business owner or facilities manager.

At the appointment, give an informal presentation on your services. Include information like the labor cost savings a lawn care or landscaping business can bring, the advantages of a well-kept lawn or other landscaping, and so on. Show pictures of residences or businesses you're currently servicing (but be sure to ask for the proprietors' permission before photographing). Mount your presentation in a sales presentation case (available at office supply stores), which has pages inside for your pictures and documents, and stands up like an easel. Stress your reliability and professionalism, offering a list of references and any earned certifications to support your reputation. Always present a business card and/or brochure.

After a few days, follow up with a phone call politely reiterating your request to serve the client. The answer won't always be "yes," but don't get discouraged.

Rejection is part of selling, and with persistence and continued professionalism, the response may one day be affirmative.

Timing Is Everything

Your main advertising campaign should be launched right before the last frost or heavy winter rains, which usually occur in late February or March. (Since meteorology isn't an exact science, try looking at seasonal weather data for the past 20 years or so to get an idea of when you can expect winter's last gasp in your region.) This is when homeowners start longing for spring and begin to make decisions about spring landscaping and mowing services. The trick is to advertise aggressively at that point and pick up enough business to carry you through the busy summer months.

Your Plan of Attack

Before you start dropping dollars on advertising of any kind, it's wise to create a basic marketing plan. This plan doesn't have to be complicated, but it should be detailed enough to serve as a road map that keeps your business on track and your marketing efforts on target. In addition, it should be updated periodically as market conditions change so you're always in touch with the needs of your customers.

Your marketing plan can be a part of the business plan you've already written. (Refer back to Chapter 5 for information about business plans.) It should describe your target market and the competitive environment you're operating in, as well as discuss how you're going to make your customers aware of your business. Information related to pricing, industry trends, and advertising also have a place in your marketing plan.

SWOT Analysis

An integral part of the marketing plan is your SWOT analysis. SWOT stands for strengths (characteristics that make you special and set you apart from the competition), weaknesses (things you need to overcome or your competitors could take advantage of), opportunities (anything you can do that might benefit your business either now or in the future), and threats (anything that can harm your business). Putting these characteristics on paper will give you a snapshot of your business's prospects.

In Figure 10–1 on page 138, we've included a sample SWOT analysis for a new lawn care business in a medium-sized urban area of about 30,000 people. Try creating your own SWOT analysis by using the blank form in Figure 10–2, page 138. You also can use the SWOT approach to analyze the strengths and weaknesses of your competition to see how you stack up against them. Once you've created your SWOT analysis, refer to it often as a guide for addressing the weaknesses you've identified and as a benchmark against which you can judge your successes.

SWOT Analysis

Strengths	Weaknesses
▶ Two summers working for a landscape contractor	▶ No experience with advertising or marketing
▶ My strong business background (B.A. in business administration)	▶ Computer-illiterate (must learn accounting software!)
▶ My strong communication skills—I can schmooze with anyone	▶ Allergic to pollen (Note to myself: See doc for allergy prescription)
Opportunities	**Threats**
▶ No other green services located within five-mile radius	▶ Commercial landscaper on Park St. has been advertising a lot and offers really low prices
▶ New condos under construction on Ferris that might be source of future income	▶ Rumors that city is considering prohibiting homebased businesses because of past abuses

FIGURE 10–1: **SWOT Analysis for a Fictional Business**

SWOT Analysis

Strengths	Weaknesses
_____	_____
_____	_____
_____	_____
_____	_____
Opportunities	**Threats**
_____	_____
_____	_____
_____	_____
_____	_____

FIGURE 10–2: **SWOT Analysis Worksheet**

Read All About It

Another important part of your marketing plan is your promotion strategy. Every horticulture professional, from the one-(wo)man band who juggles a dozen or so jobs a week to the person who needs a staff to help handle the workload, must advertise to get new business.

The types of advertising that are most effective for lawn service and landscaping companies include yellowpages.com ads, business cards, fliers, door hangers, brochures, direct mail, word-of-mouth, social media, and newspaper ads. You'll find each of these discussed below.

Social Networking

By entering contests and making your expertise public, you'll receive attention that is a natural side effect. This kind of free advertising can have powerful outcomes. You may want to create a YouTube channel that links to your website with homemade short videos offering lawn care tips. You can do this using an inexpensive digital camera with video capability. Volunteering to give informational presentations to Rotary clubs or on your public radio station can give you notoriety within your community. Look for local and national contests to enter in your field. Joining a meetup group for gardeners (www.meetup.com) will help you meet local residents who value the function and beauty of their yards. Create a Facebook (www.facebook.com) page and provide weekly green tips for your fans. You'll have to accumulate fans by socially reaching out to Facebook's audience. Volunteer to teach a class on worm casting, composting, or natural fertilizing at your local community center.

Yellow Pages Ads

Looking for a maintenance-free advertising vehicle that never closes? List your business on www.yellowpages.com, now formally known as YP. According to YP, more than 80 million people visit their site and more than 20 million businesses are listed. That said, you should always do your research and decide what advertising vehicle is best for your business in your market. "Accurate tracking is critically important and a requirement to make intelligent advertising decisions," says Blue Corona (www.bluecorona.com), a marketing solutions company. In a

> **tip** ⓘ
>
> When writing your marketing plan, think about every time you'll interact with your customers. This includes personal contact, email, and even the invoices you'll send. Each contact should be considered a potential marketing opportunity.

case study on the site the conclusion was that YP did not have a website that was worth the case study business's investment. But that doesn't mean it won't work for you!

If you use a business phone service like Fairpoint, your business will automatically be listed in their print directory, which is distributed to households in their service area.

Business Cards

Business cards are a great way to advertise at a very low cost. Those little rectangles of paper are not only your calling card—they also remind prospective customers that you're only a phone call away when he or she is ready to commit to hiring you. As a result, you should distribute your card freely wherever you go, including to anyone who should happen to walk up to you while you're on a job site with your mower in full throttle or you're wrestling a tiller through clay substrate. (Keep a supply in your truck and just a couple in your pocket, since they can get bent or soiled.)

As we mentioned in Chapter 7, these little workhorses are really quite inexpensive—starting at $15 for 1,000 cards at an office supply chain, or as little as $10, delivery included, through online printers like 123 Print (www.123print.com) or Vistaprint (www.vistaprint.com). Vistaprint has a number of free promotional products available, including business cards, rubber stamps, pens, and even websites, customized with your company information. You just pay for shipping the tangible goods and allow them to unobtrusively display their Vistaprint logo on the backside of each piece. In addition to your company name and contact information, you should use complimentary adjectives and earned credentials on your card, like "reliable" and "certified." While people usually expect you to give them an estimate without charge, printing "Free Estimates" on your cards is still a good idea because the word "free" is such a powerful motivator.

Once you have your newly printed cards, it's time to pound the pavement and get them to the masses. Set aside several hours a week for the distribution effort, and be sure to wear your company shirt or other clean, presentable attire when you canvass the neighborhoods so you look professional and competent. Never place anything in a homeowner's or business's mailbox. That is an invasion of privacy and a punishable federal offense. No kidding. And check your local regulations—some cities/towns do not allow house-to-house distribution without a permit.

Some of the potentially ripe prospects for your services include homeowners, businesses, real estate brokers, home and garden stores, and lawn mower repairpersons.

Obviously, homeowners are your biggest target market and the audience to whom you should distribute the most cards. The most direct approach for reaching them is going door to door. You don't have to knock on the door or speak to each homeowner. Just rubber band your card to the door or screen handle where it can't be missed.

If the resident comes to the door while you're doing the deed, hand the card to him or her instead and make a brief, courteous pitch about your skills and reliability. While you're at it, ask if the homeowner knows anyone who's looking for a lawn or landscaping service. That could result in an immediate job.

Be sure to have estimate forms and a measuring wheel stashed in your truck just in case the homeowner asks for an on-the-spot estimate. Never let a rich opportunity slip through your fingers by making him or her wait until you can return with the appropriate tools.

While you're out canvassing the neighborhood, be sure to stop by buildings occupied by professionals like doctors, dentists, attorneys, and insurance agents, and leave your card with their receptionists. Although these professionals may already have a service handling the lawn work, they may be in the market for someone new in the future. Ask the receptionist to keep your card on file just in case.

> ### aha!
>
> Cable TV is another place where your marketing dollars will go far. Since cable systems serve relatively small, local markets, placing an ad on the local cable station's "bulletin board" practically guarantees it will be seen by precisely the people you're trying to reach. Call the system's sales department for advertising rates before you pay to produce an ad.

Real estate brokers could be a mother lode of new, though fluctuating, lawn care business. Real estate brokers often sell homes for owners who have relocated and need a reliable mowing service—if not now, then in the future. By the same token, some real estate brokers offer relocation services and look after the homes of absentee owners. Get your cards into the hands of these brokers by stopping by in person or mailing them, along with a carefully worded sales letter. You'll find a sample letter in Figure 10–4 on page 147.

Realtors can also be a valuable source of promising landscaping leads. With the popularity of cable networks like HGTV and TLC, both of which air shows on landscaping and curb appeal, homeowners who are listing their homes or buying new ones may ask their realtor for leads to local landscaping companies. Try doing a mailing to the realtors in your target market and see what happens. (Refer back to Chapter 4 for guidance on buying mailing lists.)

They may carry a dizzying array of home and garden tools for do-it-yourselfers, but home and garden stores are still potential distribution points for your business card. Make arrangements with the store owner or manager to display your cards on the counter near the cash register for any horticulture-impaired customer who might prefer to hire a professional like you. Better yet, provide a business card holder with the cards to keep them neat and tidy on the counter.

Here's another one of those transient sources of lawn care work that really can add up to big bucks: People who take their mowers to a lawn mower repair service will be unable to tend their own lawns while the beast is out of commission—and that can be for weeks at a time during the busy season. The result? You can easily step in and cash in on an interim basis. Best of all, some of these temporary customers can turn into regulars. So stop by to introduce yourself to the lawn mower repairperson in your community and leave a supply of cards that can be distributed to mowerless customers. Look online for lawn mower repairpersons in your area. Type in the name of your city along with the words "Lawn Mowers," "Lawn Mowers—Sharpening and Repairing," "Lawn Mower Engines," and "Engines—Gasoline" to find the names of all the repair shops in your community.

Fliers

Simple to create and inexpensive to produce, fliers are probably the second hardest-working weapon in your advertising arsenal. "Every time we send fliers out, we keep busy all year," says Florida landscaper Mike Rosenbleeth. "The business kind of hits the fan."

Like business cards, fliers can be distributed widely at a fairly low cost—as little as 8 cents each when reproduced by a quickie print shop like American Speedy Printing. Fliers are generally one-sided on letter-sized paper, and can be folded and placed under windshield wipers in parking lots, posted on bulletin boards at the mall or supermarket, or distributed door to door. To increase the effectiveness of your flier, staple a business card to each one, since people are more apt to file away a business card for future reference than a piece of paper.

You can save money by using a word processing program like Microsoft Word to design the flier. Try Microsoft's online flier templates to make the job easier. Make it as appealing and easy-to-read as possible by using white space, call-outs like bullets or lists, and no more than one or two typefaces (any more than that and your flier will look like a ransom note). Among the things to

aha!

We've established that you have to stand out from the crowd and there are many ways to do that. If you're a unique landscaper, then you should have a very unique calling card. What better way to spark a potential client's interest than a scratch-n-sniff business card in the scent of hyacinth, lilac, rose, or cedar? Scent will get them thinking about their landscaping, and your professional and classy, but fun, way of approaching it may make you first in line. Check out www.promobrands.com/scratchnsniff.htm.

stress in your flier are your reliability (a BIG one), your professionalism, the conveniences you offer, and the pride customers will have when they see their beautiful yards.

It's not necessary to give prices in your flier. Generate interest by using terms like "reasonable rates," then give a phone number where you can be reached.

That Washington state lawn service owner we mentioned earlier, Lowell Pitser, uses a variation on the flier idea to informally advertise his business. He creates a "Lowell Says" flier on his home computer that gives tips on growing flowers or preventing pests, then posts them on all the free bulletin boards available in the small rural communities around his home. He says the fliers have really helped to make his name known in the community.

Michael Collins, a Michigan landscaper, is planning to make his name better known in the community by working out a deal with local realtors to put a flier into the welcome packet sent to new homeowners in his market area. The hope is that they'll give him a try simply because his company name is right in front of them, and then stay with him because of his great service. Figure 10–3 on page 144 features a sample flier.

Closely related to fliers are postcards, which, like business cards, are sometimes more likely to find their way into an address book or a day planner than a flier. They're inexpensive to print and mail, and often very effective advertising, since the message doesn't even require opening an envelope.

Door Hangers

Want to catch homeowners or office owners right where they live? Then try using door hangers, which are tags with a hole (known as a die cut) cut in the top so they can be hung from any doorknob. The standard size is 4 by 9 inches, and they can be printed in black and white or color. Obviously, the color versions are more eye-catching (especially important for a lawn and/or landscaping business), and they can be printed on UV light resistant, heavy paper to prevent damage from weather. Although they cost more than fliers, they're still quite affordable. One company we researched was running a special on 5,000 door hangers for just $190 (or 3.8 cents each), which was an outstanding deal. Typically, however, it costs about 8 to 10 cents each for 5,000 door hangers, and many companies have templates you can use to make the design

warning

You may need a permit to go door to door legally in your community. Check with the city or township clerk's office, then be sure to carry the permit in your pocket or visibly around your neck with a lanyard while you're pounding the pavement. You may have to pay a small fee for the permit.

Sample Flier

FREEDOM HILL
LANDSCAPING

For the house you love to come home to!

Reliable, reasonably priced residential services include:

- Landscaping design and installation

- Tree and shrub trimming

- Water feature and lighting installation

- Landscape maintenance

- Spring and fall cleanup

Call for a free on-site consultation and estimate.

(555) 555-5555

FIGURE 10–3: **Sample Flier**

process simple. Focal Point Communications (at www.growpro.com), which specializes in green industry marketing and advertising, features lawn and landscape graphic designs for its promotional products, including door hanger templates.

Not sure you can use that many hangers for a single campaign? Then make the copy generic—e.g., avoid promoting special sales or other dated events—and you'll be able to use the same hanger to prospect throughout your target area several times over.

We've provided contact information for a few printers who print door hangers and other promotional material under "Printing Resources" in the Appendix. However, before you spend the money and hit the streets with your smokin' hangers, check with the municipality where you're planning to start hanging to see whether a solicitor's license is required.

Brochures

Brochures are a great way to advertise your business because they give you more room to talk about your services than, say, a flier or door hanger. Brochures are also versatile. You can hand them out at home and garden shows, mail them in a No. 10 envelope to your hot prospects, or put them into a plastic brochure holder (available at office superstores) so they can be displayed at home and garden shops (but ask for permission first, of course!). Microsoft Word has many templates you can use to design your brochure, but keep in mind that even with a template, design can be tricky, and the result may not be as professional as you would like. If you'd prefer to turn the job over to a professional designer, you can expect to pay $500 or more for a trifold brochure. If that's too much for your startup budget, contact the art department at your local community college, graphic arts school, or vocational-tech program and ask for a referral to a talented student.

Unless you have creative writing skills, you may also want to hire a copywriter to write the brochure for you. This will also cost in the range of $500 to $800, depending on the writer's experience, although you can try the advertising department at local schools to see if you can find a student writer. In any event, in addition to descriptions of your services, the most important

stat fact

Great customer service opens wallets. An American Express study showed that 58 percent of consumers are willing to spend more on companies that provide excellent customer service, and a 2011 impact report commissioned by RightNow and conducted by Harris Interactive showed that 86 percent of consumers are willing to pay up to 25 percent more for a better customer experience.

tip

Use postage stamps rather than a bulk postage indicia on envelopes that contain your direct-mail offer—it makes the piece look more like personal correspondence and less like an advertising offer.

information to include in your brochure are your phone number, your brick-and-mortar address or P.O. box, and your website and/or email address so prospects can reach you immediately.

When mailing your brochure, be sure to enclose a business card in the envelope, since people are generally more inclined to file away a card for future reference than a brochure. Direct mail pros also recommend using a return address only on the outer envelope so it looks like personal correspondence rather than advertising. Finally, try including a teaser line on the outside that tempts the recipient to open the envelope and find out what's inside. A teaser that promises something free (as in "Buy one service, get one free!") or uses terms that indicate urgency ("Call now for this limited-time offer!") can induce more recipients to open up.

There are a number of online companies that will print your brochure affordably. UPrinting (www.uprinting.com) offers low-cost, do-it-yourself brochures and other custom promotional materials, with the option to proof your designs before you purchase. You can either use their online design templates or provide one of your own. For 200, 8.5-by-11-inch, trifold, double-sided, color brochures, including shipping charges, you'll pay around $115.

Direct Mail

Another way to reach potential customers right where they live is with direct mail, which is any promotional piece you send through the mail. This can include everything from brochures to newsletters and coupon books. Your direct-mail piece doesn't have to be elaborate; a simple letter (see our sample, Figure 10–4, on page 147), postcard, or flier with the appropriate hard-hitting sales copy will do. You'll also want to include a mail-back card (prepaid only—otherwise the chances of it being returned are very slim) or a business card to make it easy for your reader to contact you.

The biggest challenge with direct mail is getting the customer to open the envelope it comes in. So there are a

aha!

Sending a sales letter to your local board of realtors or chamber of commerce can be an easy way to drum up new business. Be sure to use postage on the envelopes (so they don't look like junk mail), and mail them just before the start of the mowing and planting season since this is when people will be most receptive to trying a new service.

Sales Letter

January 7, 20xx

Dear Homeowner:

It's almost spring—time to spruce up your home to make it look as fresh and beautiful as the new season. But if you're like most people, you're constantly on the go, rushing to business meetings, taking the kids to soccer and baseball practice, running errands, and doing all the other things it takes to run a career and a home. So you probably don't have as much time as you'd like to devote to the upkeep of your lawn and shrubs.

That's where Mowing Masters can help. We're a full-service lawn maintenance company located right here in your neighborhood. In addition to basic lawn mowing, we provide other quality services like hedge and bush trimming, fertilizing, thatching, and aerating—everything you need to make your home the showplace of your block.

We're experienced, reliable, and reasonably priced. You don't even have to sign a seasonal contract with Mowing Masters to get our best rates. We'll be happy to bill you monthly. And of course, your satisfaction is 100 percent guaranteed.

Please call (555) 555-5555 or visit our website (www.mowmasters.com) to set up a free estimate. Call by March 15 and you'll receive a 10 percent discount on your first month of mowing as a token of our thanks.

Sincerely,

Dan Williams

Dan Williams, Owner

25771 Regal Drive • Kissimmee, Florida 34741 • (555) 555-5555 • www.mowmasters.com

FIGURE 10–4: **Sample Sales Letter**

SPRUCE UP FOR SPRING!

$100 off any landscaping or installation project over $1,000

Expires March 31, 20XX

FREEDOM HILL LANDSCAPING
Call for free estimate: (555) 555-5555

www.FREEDOMHILLLANDSCAPING.com

FIGURE 10–5: **Sample Coupon**

few tricks you can use to incite their curiosity about the contents. One is to put the mailer in a plain No. 10 envelope that has only a return address (but no company name). This gives the envelope the appearance of personal correspondence.

Another trick that works well is using a teaser line on the envelope that piques the reader's interest. "Free" and "Increase your property value now!" are the type of teasers that would work well for a lawn care or landscaping business. As mentioned earlier, the word "free" is a powerful motivator, so offer a deal like one free mowing with a prepaid payment for three months of service or free hedge trimming with a spring cleanup worth $500 or more to encourage more people to respond.

There's one more type of direct-mail piece that bears mentioning here. That's marriage mail, which is a package that contains advertising fliers or coupons from a number of different advertisers. (ValPak is the best known in the industry.) They're usually sized to fit a No. 10 or a business-size envelope and are often printed in full color on glossy paper. (We've included a sample coupon in Figure 10–5.) The advantage is that this type of package is usually quite cost-effective, since you're only paying for a percentage of the "ride." The disadvantage is that your flier will be accompanied by other fliers from nail technicians, chiropractors, dry cleaners, and possibly other lawn or landscaping services. But the low cost usually outweighs the disadvantages. To find a company that specializes in marriage mail in your target market, search YP at www.yellowpages.com under headers like "Advertising—Direct Mail" or "Sales Promotion Service."

Word-of-Mouth

Whoever said there's no such thing as a free lunch must have overlooked word-of-mouth (WOM) advertising. Not only is the price right, but WOM praise is one of the most powerful advertising vehicles you have at your disposal. One of its major advantages is that you often don't have to do anything special to garner this kind of freebie publicity. All you do is perform your job to the best of your ability, and people will talk favorably about you and your willingness to do whatever it takes to satisfy the customer.

The key to getting good WOM is influencing what your customers say about you. You can do this in a number of ways. Some lawn service and landscaping business owners call their clients a few weeks into the mowing season or after providing a landscaping service to get feedback and verify their satisfaction. Doing this projects a positive image of you and your company because it's so rare for businesspeople in service industries to follow up after the sale. You might also get a referral or two from the satisfied homeowner during the conversation, which you can turn into a WOM opportunity by using his or her name when you call the person to whom you were referred.

Posting links on your own website to customer review sites on which you are featured encourages potential customers to read what others are saying about you. This will give also give your regular customers the idea to write their own reviews on those sites. Yelp (www.yelp.com), Angie's List (www.angieslist.com), and Viewpoints (www.viewpoints.com) are good examples of how consumers come to rely on one another's testimonials for choosing products and services.

Another way to influence WOM is by doing something positive and visible in your community or on the home and garden circuit. For example, you could present a complimentary instructional seminar on lawn care techniques for kids at the local youth center who are interested in making a few bucks mowing lawns (and who are definitely not much competition for you), and invite the local media to attend. Any coverage you get is bound to focus not only on your benevolence, but also on the services you offer. That can lead to new business.

A third way to use WOM to your advantage is to offer a referral reward program to existing customers. For instance, you could institute a "Refer a Friend" program like

> **warning**
>
> Negative word-of-mouth can be devastating for a startup business. Experts say that a dissatisfied customer might not complain to you but will tell six to seven people about the bad experience. So if you suspect that a client isn't happy with you, do whatever you can to find out why and fix the problem. The future of your business could depend on it.

Michigan landscapers Michael Collins and Karen Deighton have, which awards a $20 referral fee to current customers, or you might try giving a 10 percent discount off a month's worth of mowing for referrals made in your service area.

Newspaper Ads

You'll notice we haven't said much about newspaper advertising. Some entrepreneurs who advertise for a few weeks in the daily newspaper at the start of the mowing season feel the ads unearth some new business. But many don't think paid advertising—including classifieds—in daily newspapers is worth the cost. If your community has a free weekly shopper, you might have a go at it. The advertising in these papers tends to be quite inexpensive, and the biggest payoff seems to come from the local business and professional service section. People like to frequent the businesses in their own community and might look favorably on engaging your services.

Casting Your Net

Being online is not an option—it's an economic necessity. The internet gives us instant access to important information like NFL stats for the team that holds the record for the most consecutive games lost (Tampa Bay, 1976–77, 26 games) and shows us live cam shots of places like the summit of Alaska's Denali during a snowstorm. But more important, the internet has given us the world. We can now communicate with people 24/7, all over the planet.

According to a 2013 U.S. Census Bureau report, 83.8 percent of U.S. households had internet access with 73.4 percent reporting having a high-speed connection.

So what does this mean to you, the owner of a startup lawn care or landscaping business? It means you can get a lot of visibility without a whole lot of effort. It also means that you cannot overlook the power of the internet, both as a resource for your own business and as an electronic pathway for your customers.

So you should give very serious thought to getting a website up and running as soon as you can.

Michigan landscape company owners Michael Collins and Karen Deighton know how much value their website brings to their business. Collins says 70 percent of his snow removal customers find him online. All his other snow removal customers come to him through referrals, which just goes to show how important word-of-mouth can be, too.

This chapter will not teach you the basics of surfing the web. We will assume that you know how to log onto an ISP, use a search engine, and send and retrieve email. Instead, it will discuss how the internet can help you run your company and capture new business at the same time.

> **fun fact**
>
> Utilizing social media is still the cheapest (most often free) and fastest way to spread your reputation like wildfire. If you think you haven't got time to create a social networking profile, consider these facts from the Facebook Press Office and YouTube Press Center: YouTube receives billions of views every day. According to the Facebook newsroom, as of December 2015, there are more than 900 million active users currently accessing Facebook daily through their mobile devices.

A Phenomenal Resource

Before we delve into a discussion of using the internet as an electronic business card, we'll first explore its value as a resource and problem solver. This amazing tool can help you locate everything from advice on treating snow mold on northern lawns to the phone number of a repair shop across the country that carries a part you need right now. You have access to online auctions like eBay and resale markets like Craigslist, where you can buy just about anything you need for the business. You can do market research, investigate local zoning ordinances, and get tax help. You can accomplish all this any time of the day or night, without leaving the comfort of your home office.

Another advantage of the internet is the small-business opportunities and advice that can be accessed. There are a number of chat rooms and bulletin boards specifically for lawn care and landscaping business owners where you can share tips and trade information (we've listed a few in Chapter 9). There are also quite a few sites in cyberspace where small-business owners can find ideas to help them do business better. One to check out is *Entrepreneur* magazine's site at www.entrepreneur.com.

There's no charge for most of the wisdom out there beyond the cost of server connection fees to access the web. But remember: Sometimes you get exactly what you pay for. Just as you don't always believe everything you see in print or on the evening news, you shouldn't necessarily believe everything that's posted on the internet. After all, anyone and everyone who has the bucks to build a website, from prison inmates to the president of the Smooth River Stone Association of America, can launch themselves into cyberspace and say whatever they want. So, as the saying goes, caveat emptor, or let the buyer beware.

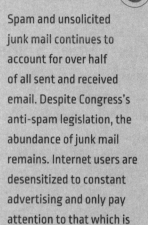

stat fact

Spam and unsolicited junk mail continues to account for over half of all sent and received email. Despite Congress's anti-spam legislation, the abundance of junk mail remains. Internet users are desensitized to constant advertising and only pay attention to that which is unique and engaging.

To protect yourself, always consider the source when searching for information, and stick with the most reputable people or companies. Let's say, for instance, you're looking for tax planning advice. You know you can trust the information you find on *Entrepreneur* magazine's site more than a website called *Manny's Guide to Beating the IRS*.

As mentioned previously, the internet is also an excellent place to start your search for lawn care and landscaping equipment and office supplies. Although not every company has its own website, there's been a huge proliferation of new websites in the past few years. As a result, it's likely you'll find the larger service companies, such as vehicle and equipment manufacturers, out in cyberspace and thus at your beck and call. (You'll find some of them listed in the Appendix and in "Straight to the Source" on page 158.)

Being connected through the internet also helps you communicate better (and often faster, since you don't waste time playing phone tag). You can place orders with suppliers, then check on their status whenever you like. You can also keep in closer touch with your customers, who may find it more convenient to email you instead of picking up the phone to tell you they'd like an extra service like fertilizing or hedge trimming.

"I often work by email with my clients," says one resourceful business owner in Ohio. "It's much easier to send off an email than to write a letter, and it's cheaper than a phone call. I may also receive an answer back the same day. You cannot beat email for efficiency."

Your Cyber Salesperson

Just as you can access other companies' websites for information about their products and services, you'll want prospective customers to find you in cyberspace, too. That means that establishing your website should be high on your list of priorities as you start your business. But you don't have to be an information technology whiz or a computer programmer to get the job done. There are many do-it-yourself web page kits on the market that almost anyone can figure out. But before we start the exciting process of building your company website, let's take a look at the website development process.

Back to Basics

Because your website is virtual advertising that's available 24 hours a day, it's important to spend a fair amount of time considering what it should say. You can do this by thinking like a customer and answering the questions you think he or she would have when searching for a lawn care or landscaping service. Here are examples of the kinds of questions your customer might have:

- ► How long have you been in business?
- ► What do you charge?
- ► Are edging and trimming included in your base lawn care rate?
- ► When will you cut my lawn (or do my landscaping) if it rains on my regularly scheduled day?
- ► What other types of services do you provide (e.g., fertilizing and chemical services)?
- ► Do you charge for estimates?
- ► How will I pay you?
- ► Do you have references?
- ► How can I reach you?
- ► How soon can you start?

Armed with answers to these questions, you should next consider how you want the site to look. It should be clean, uncluttered, and easy to use. You'll also want to keep the copy brief because many people find it annoying to have to keep scrolling down as they read. In addition, web surfers tend to have short attention spans and won't hesitate to click off your site.

▶ Work It

Here are a few other ways to use the internet:

- ▶ Seek help with lawn maintenance problems
- ▶ Learn about new trends in ornamental landscape design
- ▶ Research new mower and other product purchases
- ▶ Locate professional development courses
- ▶ Keep tabs on the competition
- ▶ Check the weather forecast
- ▶ Research turf diseases and remedies
- ▶ Purchase books and other reference/educational materials
- ▶ Buy and sell used equipment
- ▶ Create free business listings at Google My Business (for Google Search and Maps — www.google.com/places) and Yelp (www.yelp.com).
- ▶ Create affordable, targeted, pay-per-click ads, on Facebook Advertising (www.facebook.com/ads).
- ▶ Benefit from the wisdom and tutelage of mentors and online business workshops on Score (www.score.org).

Building a Better Website

The next decision you must make relates to the type of website you want to build. A simple option is the online business card, which is no more than a single screen that gives your company name and contact information like your address, phone number, and fax number. This type of website is actually quite easy to build, even for those who don't know a byte from a baud. There are many how-to internet books available in bookstores or from online retailers like Amazon that can guide you through the process of creating your own page. However, the disadvantage of this kind of web page is there's not much room for information. If you want to make a sales pitch (and why else would you go to the trouble of creating a site?), you should consider creating an online brochure instead.

With an online brochure, you can answer questions like the ones listed earlier, and provide links to your email inquiry form and other pertinent information. This is also a good way to discuss the various services you offer in detail rather than just listing them.

Another valuable thing to have on your website is a virtual portfolio that contains photographs of the work you've done. As the saying goes, a picture is worth a thousand words, and showing potential customers what you can do will be far more persuasive than telling them in words. One word of warning, however: If you can afford it, hire a professional photographer to take the photos, since he or she will show your work to its best advantage. If money is tight, you can take your own photos for now, but try to work professional grade photography into your budget as soon as possible. It doesn't come cheap, but you may find that placing a query at a local arts college may connect you with experienced photography students with lower rates who are just trying to plump up their portfolios and gain experience.

Romancing the Home(page)

By now you've probably realized that because your expertise lies in caring for plants, trees, and the green, green grass of home, you'll want to hire a professional web designer to create your website. As mentioned above, you can design it yourself using a how-to book. But unless you're well-versed in both HTML and graphic design, it's probably more trouble than it's worth, especially when there are experienced professionals out there who are awaiting your call.

Because web designers quite often are also graphic designers, they'll want you to work with them to make decisions about content, copy placement, colors, typefaces, and so on. But you can feel confident relying on the designer's best judgment when it comes to level of interactivity, navigation tools, and artwork.

Designers charge $800 to several thousands for website design. Part of this cost is based on the number of pages on the site. The more complex it is, the more it costs.

If you really think you can handle HTML and website development yourself, try using a web page layout program like Adobe Dreamweaver CC (Cloud subscription ranges from $20 to $80 per month, www.adobe.com). There are also make-your-own, free web

stat fact

Appointment-setting software saves you and your clients time and money and can glean more business for you. Nine-to-fivers typically catch up on household tasks (like making appointments) after dinner. Do you want to answer your business line at 8:00 P.M.? When you allow customers to book their own appointments on your website, you lower the risk of losing the job because of a missed call. Check out these appointment setting software packages: Genbook (www.genbook.com), Square Appointments (www.squareup.com), and TimeTrade (www. timetrade.com).

building and hosting sites that have limited capabilities, but if you just want to display some photos and contact information, they work just fine. Take a look at Weebly (www.weebly.com) and WordPress (www.wordpress.com) for ideas.

Selecting a Domain Name

Like your company, your website has to have a unique name that will be used on the server on which it resides. This is called the domain name, or URL. Examples of lawn-related domains include www.gogreenlawns.com and www.yardking.com. Using your business name as your domain name is usually your best bet, but keep in mind that domain names must be unique, and someone else might already be using the name you've chosen. Check here to see if your name has already been used by someone else: www.networksolutions.com.

> **fun fact**
>
> The extension that follows a domain name refers to the type of website it is. The ones you'll encounter most often in the green industry are: .com, which refers to commercial services; .net, which is used by networks; .org, for nonprofit organizations; .gov, for government sites; and one of the newest, .mobi, for mobile phones.

You have to register your domain name to get exclusive use of it. Domain names are registered for a minimum of two years at a fairly inexpensive cost as low as $10 per year. They can be renewed by paying another registration fee when they expire. There are several companies that handle registration, but the best-known is www.domain.com, which also allows you to register your name for five- or ten-year periods. Network Solutions boasts a $35-per-year package that includes a website, domain name, tech support, and an email address.

The Host With the Most

The last thing you have to do to go live on the net is to select an internet host site. This is where your site will reside so users can access it 24 hours a day. Examples of well-known internet hosts include MSN and EarthLink, but there are many, many smaller hosts around the country. Before selecting a host, it's a good idea to ask other businesspeople for recommendations. You'll want to know how often the host site goes down and how long it takes to fix it, how reliable its customer support is, how many incoming lines the server has (so dial-up users don't get a lot of busy signals when they call), and how big it is.

A caveat is in order here. Remember those prison inmates we mentioned earlier? Even they can be web hosts if they can somehow get the right computer equipment and

▶ Straight to the Source

Here are some websites you can use to do business better and find useful (free) advice:

- ▶ *Amazon*: sells books, CDs, videos, and more

- ▶ *Business Know-how*: interactive resource for home office and small-business owners (www.businessknowhow.com)

- ▶ *Census Bureau*: the official government website for statistics and demographics (www.census.gov)

- ▶ *Eartheasy*: solutions for sustainable living, xeriscaping and non-toxic pest control instruction (www.eartheasy.com)

- ▶ *Entrepreneur*: the premier source for small-business advice (www.entrepreneur.com)

- ▶ *FindLaw*: a free source for legal resources (www.findlaw.com)

- ▶ *GardenWeb*: interesting plant information, shopping resources, a plant exchange, and bulletin board (www.gardenweb.com)

- ▶ *Honda Power Equipment*: mowers and other power equipment (http://powerequipment.honda.com/)

- ▶ *IRS*: official source for tax tips and advice (www.irs.gov)

- ▶ *John Deere*: information about the company's walk-behind and riding mowers (www.deere.com)

- ▶ *Landscape Management*: green industry publication for landscapers (www.landscapemanagement.net)

- ▶ *Mapquest*: online driving directions in the United States (www.mapquest.com)

- ▶ *Concept Marketing Group*: has a marketing resources library with dozens of free articles of interest to small-business owners (www.marketingsource.com)

- ▶ *National Association for the Self-Employed*: offers advice, group insurance, and more (www.nase.org)

- ▶ *National Association of Enrolled Agents*: a source for locating accountants (www.naea.org)

- ▶ *National Association of Home Based Businesses*: tips and information for homebased businesses (www.usahomebusiness.com)

- ▶ *Outdoor Power Equipment Institute*: green industry-related resources and links to other useful sites (http://opei.org)

▶ **Straight to the Source,** continued

> ▶ *Scag Power Equipment*: manufacturer of commercial lawn equipment (www.scag.com)
>
> ▶ *SCORE*: free resources and counseling for small-business owners (www.score.org)
>
> ▶ *Snapper*: products and lawn care tips (www.snapper.com)
>
> ▶ *Toro*: mowers and outdoor maintenance products (www.toro.com)
>
> ▶ *United States Small Business Administration (SBA)*: the small-business owner's best friend with extensive FAQs and advice (www.sba.gov)

telephone trunk lines installed in their cell block. Unfortunately, if you take a chance with a lesser-known host, you run the risk of having it go out of business or disappear in the night, which will not inspire confidence in your customers.

Web hosting prices start as low as $19.95 per month for 20 MB of disk space. Some hosts also will allow you to register your domain name when you sign up. Web hosting is very competitive, so it pays to shop around. You'll find the names of some companies you can investigate in the Appendix.

Blowing Your Own Horn

Between your paid advertising efforts and your website, you should be able to spread the word about your new business pretty efficiently and effectively. But as you know, advertising costs money—and that's something you may not have in overabundance in the early days of your new venture.

Fortunately, there are some marketing and public relations tools you can incorporate into your promotional mix at a relatively low cost. Among these tools are newsletters, feature articles, home and garden show promotions, and networking. Here's a rundown of how each one can generate positive publicity for your business.

Newsletters

Since the advent of desktop publishing in the 1990s, it seems like everyone—from state senators to local florists—is sending out a newsletter. Newsletters are easy to create, inexpensive to produce, and very effective for delivering a copious amount of targeted information to your best prospects.

Informational newsletters tend to work well for lawn care and landscape professionals. A typical newsletter might contain checklists ("Ways to Wake Up Your Lawn This Spring"), information about the optimal time for the first spring cutting, facts about the different types of fertilizer and the importance of a regular fertilization program, information about the best way to trim hedges and shrubs, and so on. You'll want to tailor the content to reflect your business specialties, since the idea here is to sell your services subtly while providing useful tips to the prospect. You can do this by adding a tag line to the end of each newsletter story that touts your expertise. For example, on the fertilizing story, you could end with a line that says something like, "The Cutting Edge can start you on a fertilization schedule that will keep your lawn green and pristine all season long. Call (800) xxx-xxxx for a no-obligation quote."

Mailing a single newsletter just before the beginning of the growing season is sufficient for a business that focuses on mowing alone. If you also plan to do chemical applications, you might want to send another newsletter in the fall when people are starting to think about winterizing their lawns. Landscapers should make their first pitch at the end of winter to get people thinking about spring installations or renewals, and then follow up with a summer or fall newsletter, depending on what your prospects for new work are for the rest of the season.

save

Save money on newsletter design by having a graphic designer create a simple one- or two-page newsletter template that you can update yourself when you're ready to publish the next issue. Just be sure the designer uses software that's compatible with your computer system (many designers work on the Mac rather than PC platform).

Writing and Producing a Newsletter

Your newsletter should be written in a concise, journalistic style, which means each story should answer the five "W" questions (who, what, where, when, and why) and the "H" question (how). To get your message across effectively, put the most important information first. By stating "bottom line" information upfront, you're certain to hook the readers who really do have an interest in what you have to say.

► Grab Some Free Publicity

The media are always looking for interesting stories to fill space on a page or on the air, and people are always interested in services that can help make their lives easier. Keep your name out in front of them as much as you can by trying some of these less conventional strategies:

► *Become an expert.* If you have an area of expertise or a special interest in a particular aspect of horticulture, let the local media know so they can call you when they need an expert opinion. (Example: You just took a pesticide class and the local grub infestation is particularly bad this year. Don't be shy—alert the media!)

► *Make a donation.* Donate some professional time—say, a month of mowing or a flagstone patio installation—to your local public TV station for its annual auction. Or you could donate a tool or other lawn-and-garden item to be auctioned off.

► *Offer a seminar.* Spread your knowledge by teaming up with local home and garden shops, garden clubs, and other organizations to give pointers on how to make your lawn or other plantings look lush and beautiful. Don't worry about giving away trade secrets and losing business. There will be enough people there who won't have a clue what you're talking about, or might not have the inclination to put your ideas into practice. Then, bingo—you end up with more viable leads.

► *Support your community.* Donate materials or time to help a local environmental group or garden club. Your benevolence will resonate throughout the community.

► *Take up a cause.* Actively supporting environmental protection can put you in the spotlight. But avoid controversial issues and politics. Whichever side you take, you'll alienate the people who support the other side.

If writing newsletter stories sounds like too daunting a task, consider hiring a freelance writer to produce the copy for you under your guidance. Good sources for finding freelance help include local professional advertising organizations, your local chamber of commerce, and university journalism programs. You can expect to pay $350 to $800 for a four-page newsletter, depending on the experience of the writer. You also could use a marketing firm, but that can be pretty expensive for a new business owner.

The standard size for a newsletter is 8.5 by 11 inches. It's usually produced in multiples of four pages, but there's absolutely no reason why you can't do a two-pager, which is a single sheet with type on the front and back. It's usually easy to come up with enough copy to fill a two-page newsletter, and it will keep your costs down since it can easily be produced on a photocopier and mailed in a No. 10 business envelope. To save money, you could email your newsletter instead, but keep in mind that not all people are willing to open email attachments, which means all your hard work might end up in the virtual trash.

After the copy has been written, it has to be placed into position on the newsletter pages. There are a number of affordable software packages available to help you do this yourself. Many of them come with newsletter templates that allow you to type in headlines and paste in copy blocks, and the program does the copy fitting and formatting. A reasonably priced desktop package you can try is Microsoft Publisher 2016 at $110. Microsoft Word also comes with a newsletter template, but keep in mind that if you use it, your newsletter might look exactly like the one produced by the local elementary school, Catholic church, Feng Shui practitioner, and so on.

It's perfectly acceptable to design your newsletter with all words and no artwork. But clip art is so inexpensive and easy to use that it makes sense to buy an all-purpose clip art package that includes lawn and garden art. (Don't forget that you can use the clip art on other promotional materials you create, too, including fliers.) A good clip art package to try is ClickArt Premiere Image Pak from Broderbund offering hundreds of thousands of clip art for $10 or $20, depending on where you purchase it. If you own Microsoft Office, you automatically have access to a nice selection of lawn and garden clip art you can use. Although photographs can really make a newsletter look great, don't use them if you're planning to photocopy it. The reproduction quality will be terrible, which will diminish your newsletter's appearance overall.

If you don't feel up to the task of designing your newsletter, hire a freelance designer. You can expect to pay up to $500 (or $30 to $60 per hour) for a designer's services.

Feature Articles

Feature stories are an excellent way to garner publicity for your business. What makes these articles such powerful and effective tools is the fact that they can be used to position you as an authority in your field. That's a great way to gain credibility while building a solid reputation as a savvy businessperson.

Feature stories can run the gamut from informational articles to profiles about your company. The slant you take depends on the type of publication to which you're planning to submit the article. For instance, a story on "The Top 10 Reasons to Hire a Landscaper" might be perfect for the features section of your daily newspaper. On the other hand, an article about your entrepreneurial talents or your successful business startup might be more appropriate for the business section of your paper or a specialty business magazine.

Don't overlook the value of sharing your knowledge and insight with readers. The idea is to "wow" them with your expertise so they immediately think of you when they're ready to engage someone to take over the lawn care duties at their home, or to turn their yards into masterpieces of landscape design. Write articles giving tips for cultivating a beautiful, lush lawn. Share stories about fertilizing disasters and how they can be fixed or avoided. Or report on the innovative and unusual landscaping you installed for the city's leading citizen. The possibilities are endless.

Although feature articles can run anywhere from 800 to 2,500 words, depending on the publication, a reasonable length is 1,000 to 1,200 words. As with newsletters, you can use a freelance writer to "ghostwrite" or produce the articles under your byline. You can expect to pay a freelance ghostwriter about $350 to $750 for a 1,200-word article.

> ### aha!
>
> If you're going after commercial business, you should consider packaging all of your promotional and sales materials in a media kit, which can be distributed to business prospects. Some of the items in the kit (which are usually organized in a pocket folder) may include a letter thanking the client for his or her interest, some background information about the business, copies of any articles in which you've been quoted (or are the star of), a brochure or flier, and your qualifications (including chemical certifications).

Submitting Your Manuscript

The article manuscript should be double-spaced on letter-sized white bond paper with one-inch margins on all sides. Send the article with a pitch letter that briefly describes what the article is about and why it would appeal to the readers of the publication. Always remember to give information about how and where you can be reached at the end of the article.

Locating the right recipient for the article is a cinch. You can either call the chosen magazine or newspaper to find out the name of the appropriate person, or check the publication's website for a list of editorial staff members. Never address your story to "Editor" or, worse yet, just the name of the publication. It's far less likely to get to the appropriate person that way. A few days after you've mailed the article, follow up with the editor by phone.

Home and Garden Show Promotions

For sheer numbers, there may be no better place to gain quick exposure for your business than a consumer home and garden show. These events attract hundreds or even thousands of homeowners—people who, by their presence alone, are announcing loudly and clearly that they're interested in the services you offer.

Home and garden shows are generally held in convention centers in large cities. For a fairly reasonable price, you can rent booth space in these shows. Then it's up to you to chat up prospective customers, cheerfully hand out your business card and services list, and otherwise lay the groundwork that will result in new business.

If you've ever been to a trade show of any kind before, you know that some companies set up elaborate booths with fancy graphics and high-tech lighting. But don't feel like you have to go this route, too. After all, you're a small-business owner, and as such, you're probably not in a position to drop thousands of dollars on a booth you'll use just a few times a year. So instead, put on a shirt with your company logo and accessorize it with a big smile. Once you start talking to people, no one's even going to notice your modest booth space with its 10- or 12-foot skirted table.

One thing they will notice, however, is any giveaway items you have. You definitely will want to spring for at least one novelty item since you'll be competing with other companies that offer the same kinds of products and services. Specialty items like pens, nail files, refrigerator magnets, and other gizmos that are personalized with the name and address of your business are great giveaways. The hope is, of course, that every time the prospect picks up the item, he or she will be reminded of your business and will one day call for an estimate.

tip

Calendars make a particularly good giveaway item, given the seasonality of your business. If you can afford them, small pocket-sized calendars are a good choice because people tend to carry them around and pull them out of pockets and purses for all to see.

Advertising specialty items (known as "trinkets and trash" in the biz) are surprisingly inexpensive. For example, 500 stick pens personalized with your company name cost roughly $150 and 500 business card magnets are around $110 at Big Promotions. If an item—any item—can be imprinted, there's probably a specialty promotional company that carries it. Try Blueberry Ink for more promotion items (see the Appendix for contact information).

tip

Don't just exchange pleasantries and business cards when you network at professional business organization meetings. Plan a follow-up meeting with people whose interests mesh with yours or might even be potential clients. Just be sure to make a notation on the back of their cards so you'll remember why you're pursuing the relationship.

Prize drawings are an effective way to attract people to your booth. The prize should be something lawn care- or landscaping-related that would be perceived as valuable to this audience, like a month's worth of free mowing or one power raking. Prepare entry forms in advance (you can create them six to a page using your home computer, then have the pages photocopied at a quick print shop and cut into individual forms), and bring a big fishbowl or another container to collect them. Then when people come up to fill out the entry forms, start a conversation to find out whether they're in your target market, and if so, pitch them for all you're worth.

Even if you don't come away with any firm commitments from the people in attendance, you'll still have something very valuable as a result of your efforts: a fishbowl full of leads that you can use to send out direct-mail advertising or a newsletter you've developed especially for this purpose.

Some of the major national home and garden shows in the United States are listed in the Appendix under "Home and Garden Shows."

Networking

You know the old saying: It's not what you know, but who you know. The more people you know, the easier it will be to drum up new business.

Two extremely valuable networking sources are your local chamber of commerce and Rotary Club. These organizations consist of both small and large business owners, and encourage their members to exchange ideas, support each other's businesses, and barter services. The cost to join either organization is reasonable, and you can quickly build a reputation as a caring and reputable business owner by becoming involved in the groups' public service activities. More important, you can network on a regular basis with other business owners who personally may need green services, or know someone who does.

Finally, professional lawn care and landscaping service organizations are a good place to meet other business owners and share tips and techniques. Many of the national organizations have regional chapters that hold regular meetings.

The Green Stuff

Well, you've certainly accomplished a lot if you've made it this far. Hopefully, the prospects of starting up a green business are looking pretty promising to you right now. But there's one teensy little thing you still have to work out. There's a maintenance issue that can make or break your business; namely, long-term financial management.

Did you just turn pale and look heavenward for help? If so, you are not alone. Many of us make certain career choices because we're not as interested in or adept at other ones. Though you can turn grass a mean shade of green and artfully sculpt shrubbery, you may not be comfortable with balance sheets and cash flow statements. This doesn't mean you can't learn how to do it. At the very least you need to know how much money is coming in and how much is going out, and to do that you need to have patience, perseverance, and maybe a software package or two to keep those numbers on your financial statements in the black.

Anyone who's been in this business for a while will tell you that one of its main challenges (aside from avoiding nitrogen burnout and dodging pesky dogs) is being able to stash away enough "scratch" during your busy season to keep you afloat during the lean days of winter. Even if you live in a part of the country where winters are mild, such as Florida, you'll still experience times when revenues are slimmer. (For instance, some of those snowbirds who fly down from the northern states may be tempted to do some of the yard work themselves, thus impacting your revenue stream.) Planning for such eventualities is key to weathering the slow times in this seasonal industry.

In this chapter, we'll discuss the tools of financial management and how to calculate the amount of money you'll need to carry you through the off-season.

Income and Operating Expenses

In Chapter 6, we mentioned the value of a good accountant who can help you through the wonders of corporate bookkeeping. But you still must know enough about your own business situation to understand what he or she is doing to keep you honest in the eyes of the IRS and your creditors.

One tool you'll need is a simple income/operating expenses (I&E) worksheet like the one shown in Figure 13–2 on page 174 that will help you estimate your monthly expenses. The sample statements in Figure 13–1, starting on page 172, show the operating costs for two hypothetical lawn and landscaping service businesses—one whose owner handles all the work alone, and another whose owner has a part-time employee. Not all the expenses shown will apply to you, but they give

save

To save on overhead costs, keep your business at home as long as possible—if not forever. If you need more room, convert part of your attic or basement into a work area, then reorganize your belongings, rid yourself of clutter, and store what you don't need offsite. That's much more cost-effective than renting a commercial office space.

a rundown of the typical expenses a lawn care service or landscaping professional can expect to incur.

The sample income/operating expense statements for two hypothetical businesses that reflect typical operating costs for the lawn and landscaping industries follow on pages 172 and 173. The low-end business, The Yard Man, is a part-time lawn business that services 32 clients per week. The high-end business, Freedom Hill Landscaping, is a landscape maintenance sole proprietorship with one part-time assistant (20 hours per week). It offers landscape design, installation, and maintenance.

Please note that not every expense discussed in this chapter appears on these sample I&Es; we've made some assumptions about what each company's monthly expenses might be simply to give you an idea of how you can structure your own expense statement. After reviewing these costs, you can try computing your own projected income and expenses using the worksheet provided in Figure 13–2 on page 174.

Phone/Utilities

Assuming you have a business telephone line, you can note the average monthly cost of the bill on your I&E. However, as we mentioned in a previous chapter, business lines can be very costly—from $150 to as much as $400 per line vs. $30 to $40 per month for basic residential services. For this reason, some entrepreneurs choose to install a second residential line and use it exclusively for the business. If you go that route, the total cost would be completely deductible. But a word of advice: If you use your home phone number to make occasional long-distance business calls, be sure to keep a handwritten log of business calls that you can compare against your phone bill every month. The IRS usually requires written records for any expenses you deduct, and it will be much easier to determine which calls are legitimate business expenses if you have a log to refer to.

As you no doubt know, there are many add-on phone services that can be useful for a homebased business owner. At $15 to $20 per line, voicemail is a bargain, as is call waiting ($5-$8 per month) and caller ID (about $9 for number ID and $2 extra for name display). Some phone companies include many of these features (and a certain number of long-distance minutes) in their basic phone packages, so it pays to shop around for a bundled telecom package.

> **tip** (i)
>
> Bankers look at three measures to determine your business's ability to make a profit: the gross profit margin, operating profit margin, and net profit margin. The decision to lend is made based on this information because it's the best indication of whether you're a good financing risk.

Sample Income/Operating Expenses

The Yard Man		
Projected Monthly Income		**$3,000**
Projected Monthly Expenses		
Phone (office and cell)	$80	
Postage	$75	
Office supplies	$25	
Licenses	$5	
Owner salary	$1,800	
Employee wages		
Benefits/taxes (10% of wages)		
Workers' comp		
Advertising/promotion	$90	
Insurance	$25	
Legal services	$75	
Accounting services	$160	
Online service	$20	
Web hosting	$15	
Merchant account		
Transportation/maintenance	$100	
Publications/dues	$26	
Loan repayment		
Miscellaneous	$240	
Total Expenses	**$ 2,736**	
Projected Profit		**$ 264**

FIGURE 13–1: **Sample Income/Operating Expenses**
Study this example of two I&E statements from our fictional high-end and low-end companies.

Sample Income/Operating Expenses

Freedom Hill Landscaping		
Projected Monthly Income		$5,300
Projected Monthly Expenses		
Phone (office and cell)	$80	
Postage	$75	
Office supplies	$25	
Licenses	$5	
Owner salary	$2,000	
Employee wages	$800	
Benefits/taxes (10% of wages)	$80	
Workers' comp	$25	
Advertising/promotion	$160	
Insurance	$25	
Legal services	$75	
Accounting services	$ 160	
Online service	$40	
Web hosting	$15	
Merchant account	$30	
Transportation/maintenance	$100	
Publications/dues	$50	
Loan repayment	$800	
Miscellaneous	$455	
Total Expenses	**$ 5,000**	
Projected Profit		**$ 300**

FIGURE 13–1: **Sample Income/Operating Expenses**

Income/Operating Expenses Worksheet

Projected Monthly Income		$
Projected Monthly Expenses		
Phone (office and cell)	$	
Postage	$	
Office supplies	$	
Licenses	$	
Owner salary	$	
Employee wages	$	
Benefits/taxes (10% of wages)	$	
Workers' comp	$	
Advertising/promotion	$	
Insurance	$	
Legal services	$	
Accounting services	$	
Online service	$	
Web hosting	$	
Merchant account	$	
Transportation/maintenance	$	
Publications/dues	$	
Loan repayment	$	
Miscellaneous	$	
Total Expenses	$	
Projected Profit		$

FIGURE 13–2: **Income/Operating Expenses Worksheet**

Finally, your cell phone costs can be included in your monthly expenses if the phone is used strictly for business. The IRS is quite clear about what constitutes a legitimate business expense, and a phone that's used to order Chinese takeout or check in with the babysitter does not qualify for the deduction. If your cell phone is used more for pleasure than business, you should leave it out of your calculation on your I&E.

warning

It's important to take a regular salary—no matter how small—just as soon as your revenue can support one. Otherwise, you won't be able to prove your income to a bank or other lender when you want to buy a car, buy a house, or borrow cash for any other worthwhile purpose.

Postage

As mentioned in Chapter 10, you may want to do a mass mailing a few times a year to drum up new prospects. Estimate your postage costs here. Also, if you anticipate having any monthly shipping charges, include those, too.

Wages

It's pretty common for startup lawn care and landscaping business owners to plunge all their initial earnings back into the business rather than taking a salary for themselves. If you're starting a full-time business meant to support yourself and your family, that isn't an option. But if your startup is part time, then putting all the profits back into the business can be a savvy business move. Consider the market, how much the average lawn or landscaping service costs, and how many services you'll be able to provide as a one-(wo)man band to arrive at a loosely projected annual income, and then divide that figure by 12 to arrive at a number for your I&E.

As far as employee wages are concerned, you'll want to pay enough to keep your helpers from job jumping the moment someone else offers 25 cents more per hour. Because of the skill necessary to trim and edge and do other lawn and landscaping tasks, it's a good idea to pay better than minimum wage, as Steve Mager in Minnesota does. Colorado landscaper Kelly Giard's commission system allows workers to potentially earn much more than that. His best people earn between 30 to 35 percent of each sale. Most of the entrepreneurs interviewed for this book pay their employees much more than the current federal minimum wage. (Wages of $12 or more per hour are pretty common in the industry.)

For the sake of our sample I&E in this chapter, we've included wages for a 20-hour-per-week part-time lawn maintenance employee at $10 an hour.

Advertising

Include the cost of fliers and other advertising you may decide to do. A generally accepted rule of thumb for estimating advertising costs is to set aside 3 to 5 percent of your annual revenues for business promotion. So let's say you expect to pull in first-year part-time revenues of $25,000. You should spend $750, or 3 percent, of that money on advertising, which works out to $62.50 a month, which will buy you a lot of fliers.

Insurance

Using the worksheet in Figure 6–1, page 81, in Chapter 6, tally up the amount of insurance you plan to carry, including the cost to insure the truck or van you'll use to transport yourself, your crew, and your equipment to job sites. As with the phone expenses, you should only note business-specific expenses. If you also use your vehicle to transport the kids to a ballgame or to go shopping, you'll have to estimate what percentage of the vehicle is actually used for your business and then apply that to your insurance cost to arrive at a usable number. One reliable way to do this that the IRS will find acceptable is to keep a simple mileage log. Office supply stores sell mileage log books that are small enough to stash in your glove compartment or a pocket of your visor. Make sure you jot down both business and personal mileage every time you get behind the wheel, or your records won't be acceptable to the IRS.

Legal Services

As you'll recall from Chapter 6, it's usually advisable to include an attorney on your business team, especially since you'll be working with customers whose actions cannot always be predicted. (People have been known to sue for far less than fertilizer burn or birdhouse breakage.) Unfortunately, it can be a little tricky to estimate upfront just how much your monthly legal expenses may be beyond the cost of incorporation and/or other basic services. Consult your attorney to find out whether he or she works either by the hour or on retainer. If the former, it's a breeze to estimate the number of hours you'll need and arrive at a number for your I&E. If the latter, you can simply divide the retainer fee by 12 to arrive at a figure. On the other hand, if you're

save

Self-employed persons can deduct 100 percent of their health insurance premiums on their taxes. You can take this deduction even if you don't qualify for the itemized medical deduction, and it comes off your total income, not your adjusted gross income, which saves you even more money.

▶ Check Up

If you're planning to accept personal checks from your customers, you should subscribe to a check verification service. Such services maintain nationwide databases of more than one million checking accounts and will alert you if your customer has written bad checks. The service will also tell you if there have been an unusually large number of checks written on the account, which could be an indication of fraud. The cost of a verification service is similar to that of a merchant account and usually includes a discount fee on all checks you process and a per-item transaction fee of 15 to 25 cents. Additional fees may include a monthly minimum fee, a statement fee, and an application fee. But it's worth it because you get the best possible verification that every check you accept is good. To get the best software for your business, see www.possoftwareguide.com/articles/news94.html.

only planning to pay for a startup package, you can leave the legal line blank at this time. You can easily add funds later if unexpected legal fees crop up. For the sake of simplicity on our sample I&E, we've used a figure of $75, which works out to $900 a year and should cover basic services.

Accounting Services

This cost is easier to estimate since accountants often work on an hourly basis. You can check with your own accountant for guidance, but it's probably safe to assume that you'll have no more than three to five hours of work a week, depending on how complex your finances are. (Karen Deighton in Michigan, who is a controller by trade, says she spends about three hours a week on the books in a typical week.) According to the *Occupational Outlook Handbook*, 2014, the median salary for an accountant was $65,940 in 2014, which works out to $31.70 an hour. We've rounded that figure up to $32 an hour and plugged $160 into our sample I&E for five hours of work per month.

Transportation/Maintenance

Keeping your equipment in good working order is paramount, or you'll be out of business if it's not. Tally up the cost of regular tune-ups for both your power equipment and vehicle, then add an amount to cover regular maintenance like oil changes, spark plug replacement, and blade sharpening. To that add the estimated cost of gasoline, windshield wiper fluid, travel-related costs, and vehicle payments if appropriate.

Magazine Subscriptions

As mentioned in Chapter 9, there are many green savvy publications to mentor your technical, networking, and cutting-edge industry education. The two places to account for them are your startup worksheet and your I&E, on which you divide by 12 for the monthly expense. Budget a few extra bucks for business reference books, including green-related volumes or general business practice guides. That extra amount—$10 or $20 a month—can be added to your publications cost figure.

Membership Dues

Since membership in industry and professional organizations can be really beneficial for a startup entrepreneur, you should earmark funds to pay for those memberships. Refer back to Chapter 9 and see the Appendix for a range of industry-specific organizations that might be of interest to you. Tally their annual dues, divide that amount by 12, and include that figure here.

save

It's not necessary to use a receipt printer when you process credit card payments, although it will look more professional to the customer if you can present a printed receipt. A neat handwritten receipt written on a form created for that purpose is acceptable, especially when you're working out in the field.

Loan Repayment

If you had to finance capital expenditures like trucks or trailers, lawn and landscaping equipment like riding mowers, or home office equipment like computers, you'll note the monthly loan payment here. If you happen to be using a family vehicle for the business, figure out the percentage of business use, multiply that by your payment, and place the resulting figure on this line.

Office Supplies

This includes all the paper clips, stationery, business cards, and other supplies you need to do business every day. Obviously, some expenses like business printing won't be incurred every month, so use the figures you got when you priced your business cards and divide by 12. This number gets added to the other costs you've estimated for the month.

Merchant Account

It's becoming a common practice for small-business owners of all types to offer their customers the option of paying with credit and debit cards, especially since the total amount of some landscaping services can be in the thousands. Even lawn care maintenance business owners who invoice on a monthly basis find it's a good idea to take plastic. To do so, you'll need what's known as a merchant account. Simply stated, a merchant account is an electronic payment clearinghouse. For a set monthly fee and a whole bunch of transaction fees (which we'll get to later), you can check a person's credit or debit his or her checking account, and you'll have the money in your own business checking or savings account in just a few days.

To use a merchant account, you'll need a phone connection (your business line will do nicely), and a point-of-sale (POS) terminal and credit card receipt printer. Then you simply swipe the customer's credit or debit card through the reader and wait for an approval code. Alternatively, you can purchase software that can be used with your computer for clearing payments, but

stat fact

Showing a 10 to 20 percent net profit is a good indication that your company is healthy and prospering. Don't be concerned if it takes you a while to achieve that level; the most important thing is to show progress toward that goal because it means both you and your bills are getting paid.

you need a computer and an internet connection (wireless if you're out in the field) to do so. (Refer back to Chapter 7 for a more in-depth discussion of the alternatives, such as the Square card swiper, a whole new way of processing credit cards.)

This is a great system that guarantees that the customer's credit is good, but we'll admit it comes at a rather high cost. The costs you'll incur include a discount rate paid on each transaction, which amounts to a fixed percentage deducted from each purchase by the merchant account provider. This fee can range anywhere from 1.5 to 4 percent per transaction. Most merchant account providers also typically charge a $10 statement fee each month, as well as a small fee for each transaction processed (usually around 20 cents). Other costs may include a programming charge to set up your account, a monthly minimum fee, a "gateway" fee for secure payments, a chargeback processing fee—and the list goes on. The good news is, the merchant account business is fairly competitive, and providers usually offer a variety of fee options and combinations to attract your business. So it really does pay to shop around. You'll find a list of merchant account providers in the Appendix as a starting point, or you can do a merchant account search on the internet to unearth tons more. In the meantime, for the purpose of your I&E statement, you can use a figure of around $30 as an estimate of your startup merchant account fees.

Benefits/Taxes

As we mentioned in Chapter 8, offering benefits can be a great way to attract qualified workers and keep them happy when they're on board, both of which are important since it can be difficult to find good help and train them appropriately. But as a fledgling entrepreneur, you may find it's out of your budget to offer perks like health insurance and a 401(k) retirement plan. If you choose to offer benefits, you will enter the cost here. But if you're like many business owners, you may find it more cost-effective to offer a week of paid vacation or a few personal days instead. If you take the latter route, you can simply skip ahead to the taxes line, where you definitely will have an entry to make.

As we discussed in Chapter 8, employers are responsible for a whole wheelbarrow full of taxes, including taxes collected from your employees and taxes you pay for your employees. Among these taxes are FICA, Medicare, Federal Unemployment Tax, state unemployment tax, and workers' compensation insurance. Unfortunately, there's no simple calculation for estimating these taxes, and since you don't have any previous records, making a good guess is that much more difficult. Ask your accountant to help you come up with an estimated monthly amount for your I&E so you don't end up way off base on those monthly projections.

If you're using contract help (e.g., anyone not paid out of your payroll account), it's not necessary to collect or pay taxes because they're responsible for covering their own tax liabilities, including both sides of the FICA tax (aka Social Security). Your responsibility is limited to issuing a 1099 form at the end of the year to any subcontractor who earns more than $500 from you. That might sound great, but just remember what we said in Chapter 8 about Uncle Sam's definition of subcontractors. If a person works in your office, is under your direct supervision, or meets a host of other requirements, that person is considered an employee, and you're liable for all those taxes mentioned above. For guidance, review IRS Publication 15-A, *Employers' Supplemental Tax Guide*, which discusses the employee/independent contractor distinction, or speak to your accountant.

As a self-employed person and sole proprietor, you have your own set of taxes to be concerned with. For starters, you'll have to pay estimated taxes on a quarterly basis. For this reason, you must keep careful records, because if you miss a payment or mail it in after the due date, it will catch up with you at tax time, and you're liable to be stuck with a late-payment penalty. That really hurts as your income increases and is another example of why you need an accountant to accurately forecast how much you'll owe. If cash flow isn't a problem (unlikely) and you prefer to go it alone (unwise), you could try projecting your income for the quarter and multiplying that figure by .40 (40 percent). Next, figure out your state and/or local government's tax bite, and then send all the rest to the Fed. If you do business in a state with an especially high income tax rate (like Vermont, at 8.95 percent in 2015), you might need to estimate even higher. Are you appalled at that figure?

It's because as a self-employed person, you're paying a self-employment tax equal to both sides of the Social Security tax and Medicare, exactly the same way your contractors must. Is your business an S corporation? Then get ready for more fun. You still have to pay estimated taxes on any money you earn, even if all the money stays in the corporation. But take heart—it would be worse if it wasn't for the Jobs and Growth Tax Relief Reconciliation Act of 2003, which reduced the top corporate tax rate from 38.6 percent to 35 percent.

Of course, all is not lost. As a business owner, you'll be able to deduct expenses that will help offset those obnoxious tax bills. One important deduction you can take is for mileage to and from job sites. In 2015, the business mileage deduction was 57.5 cents per mile. It's usually best to write off your mileage on Schedule C of your taxes (if you're a sole proprietor) rather than charging your customers, since they could perceive an extra charge as outrageous, and that could prompt them to look for another service provider closer to home. In any event, if you feel you must charge for mileage because of high fuel prices, you might want to build the cost into your rate quietly rather than itemizing it as a separate expense. The sole exception to this would be if a client were located so far outside your normal service area that the cost of getting there would seriously undermine your profit margin. If the client were that serious about having you do the work, he or she may be equally serious about getting you out there no matter what the cost.

Additional business deductions may be taken for anything you use solely for the job, like power equipment, tools, office equipment, and supplies. Your vehicle and the cost to operate it (oil changes, maintenance, and so on) also are deductible expenses. However, if you use your personal vehicle, computer, etc., for the business, your uncle in Washington will only let you deduct the amount equal to the percentage these things are used for business. That's why keeping detailed written records of every transaction and every mile driven is critical.

It should be pretty obvious by now that tax issues are fairly complex. For this reason, we strongly recommend that you hire an accountant. The cost of using an expert (also deductible, by the way) is worth it when you consider how much you stand to save in late penalty and underpayment fees.

save

The IRS permits small-business owners to deduct 50 percent of qualifying expenses for travel, meals, and entertainment, which may come in handy when you travel to trade shows—but doesn't apply when you stop at McDonald's for lunch in between jobs. To take the deduction, you'll need receipts or other proof substantiating the amount claimed.

Miscellaneous Expenses

Other incidentals like herbicides for spraying cracks in the sidewalk or trash bags for your clipping collection are added in here. Adding 10 percent to your bottom line total to cover incidentals usually works well.

Receivables

Here's where the fun begins. Hopefully, the money you receive from your clients will offset all the operating expenses you just read about and leave you with a little change to jingle in your pocket that will carry you through the entire year. But the only way you'll know where you stand is by keeping careful records of your receivables.

We've provided a receivables worksheet in Figure 13–3, page 183, that you can use to track the fruits of your labor. You can either reproduce the sheet provided there or customize your own using a standard accountant's columnar pad available at any office supply store. These pads come with two to 12 or more columns to keep your accounting tidy. Usually, a six-column pad will do the job nicely. It's low-tech, but it works for people who are not computer literate or are too busy to learn. If you decide to invest in an accounting software package (discussed in further detail later in this chapter), you can log your receivables right on your computer and always have a running total available.

tip

A handshake is the preferred "contract" for most lawn care and many landscaping professionals. But if you'll be doing large-scale commercial work, you should draw up a written contract that spells out your responsibilities and payment terms. Under the Uniform Commercial Code, contracts for the sale of services or goods in excess of $500 must be in writing to be legally enforceable.

Paying the Piper

Before you can line your pockets with silver, you'll have to bill your clients regularly. You'll find a sample invoice you can adapt to your specifications in Figure 13–4 on page 184. All the lawn and landscape entrepreneurs we spoke to said they bill monthly, and most use some kind of business software to do the job. No matter how you bill, make sure you get those invoices mailed out at the same time each month, like around the 1st or the 15th. In addition to keeping your cash flow flowing, sending bills on a regular schedule will get your customers accustomed to seeing your bill at a certain time, and hopefully, they'll work it into their monthly budgets.

Receivables Worksheet

Receivables Year _____

Date Posted	Client	Amount	Check #	Balance Due

FIGURE 13–3: **Receivables Worksheet**

Sample Invoice

July 30, 20XX   Terms: Net 30

Sold to:

    David Mower
    49855 Petrucci Dr.
    Lake Buena Vista, FL 55555

    Mowing and edging service for July 20xx

    4 weeks @ $20 per cut $80

    Fertilizing (3rd seasonal application) @ $31/application $31

    Total   **$111**

Thank you!

25771 Regal Drive • Kissimmee, Florida 34741 • (555) 555-5555 • www.mowmasters.com

FIGURE 13–4: **Sample Invoice**

High-Tech Bookkeeping Solutions

Accounting and business software has become so user-friendly and affordable that practically anyone can use it, including people who are bookkeeping challenged. The hands-down choice of the lawn care and landscaping pros we interviewed was QuickBooks by Intuit. QuickBooks Pro standalone desktop software retails for $199.95 and is sold at office supply and computer stores everywhere. It allows you to create invoices, track receivables, write checks, pay bills, and more. It also interfaces with Microsoft Word, Excel, and other software. Another plus: Data from QuickBooks can be imported directly into income tax preparation packages like TurboTax if you're brave enough to do your own business or personal taxes (not recommended if your tax situation is complex).

save

A cost-effective way to get the equipment you need for a particular job is to rent or lease it. There's no point in buying a big-ticket item like a rototiller if you're only going to use it a couple of times a year. Simply roll the cost of the rental into any estimate you prepare.

Another popular accounting package you might like to try is Sage Pro Accounting. It retails for $60 and is available online from computer stores and directly from Sage (www. sage.com).

One of the best reasons to use accounting software is because it prevents inadvertent math errors. All you have to do is plug in the correct numbers and they're crunched appropriately.

Where the Money Is

You now have all your ducks in a row. Your business plan is exemplary, and you have solid evidence that your community or metropolitan area has the well-heeled economic base necessary to support your fledgling business. So business financing should be a snap, right? In your dreams. Small-business owners sometimes discover it's pretty hard to find a bank willing to work with them. This is usually because the mega-rich banks are a lot more interested in funding large companies that need lots of capital. They're also leery about dealing with one-person and startup companies. So it may be hard to find the financing you need to buy reliable mowing or landscaping equipment.

One way around this problem is to shop around to find a bank that will actually welcome the opportunity to work with you. "Community banks and credit unions may serve as your . . . best bet," says Julian Hills in "How to Finance a Startup Today" (www.

entrepreneur.com/article/229459). "Since many community banks avoided the housing crisis, they'll often have money to lend without the same standards as national banks. Local small businesses are finding success with community banks if they can convince leaders they'll make a profit and pay back the loans."

You probably already have a pretty good idea who the smaller banking players are in your community. Start by checking out their annual reports, which are usually readily available at branch offices, for clues about their financial focus and business outlook. Important clue: Institutions that support minority- and women-owned businesses as well as small businesses are likely to be more willing to help your small business (even if you personally are not a minority or a woman). Next, look for information about the number of loans the banks make to small companies. That's a pretty good indicator of their community commitment. Finally, study their overall business mix and the industries they serve.

While it's not impossible to find a big bank that will welcome you into the financial fold, it's actually far more likely that warm welcome will come from a smaller financial institution. According to consultants at the Michigan Small Business Development Center at the One Stop Capital Shop in Detroit, small banks traditionally are better for small businesses because they're always looking for ways to accommodate these customers, they're more willing to deal with small-business concerns, and they're more sensitive to issues like the need for longer accounts receivable periods. Need some ideas? Visit www.entrepreneur.com/bestbanks for a list of small-business-friendly banks.

Uncle Sam to the Rescue

Even if you find a bank that's friendly to small business, you may still have trouble establishing credit or borrowing money as a startup business. Banks both large and small are always more reluctant to part with their cash when the business owner doesn't have a proven track record.

That's where agencies like the SBA can help. It offers a number of free services to small-business owners, including counseling and training seminars on topics like business plan and marketing plan development. The idea is to help the owner understand what the bank will want from him or her before ever setting foot inside the front door.

The SBA also offers a number of different loan programs, counseling, and training. For more information, check the SBA's website at www.sba.gov, email answerdesk@sba.gov, or call (800) UASK-SBA.

▶ Take Some Credit

Financing your lawn care or landscaping business startup with your personal credit cards can save you both the hassle of applying for a bank loan and the hefty costs that can be associated with it. The downside is that you'll probably pay interest rates of as much as 24.9 percent. If you decide to use plastic, use a card with the lowest interest rate. Keep checking your mailbox for low-rate offers. There are even zero percent offers out there, which is much appreciated by business owners who are just starting out.

If your credit is good, you may be able to obtain a separate small-business line of credit through your credit card company. This allows you to borrow as much as $25,000 with no other costs than an application fee and at a rate that's probably a lot less than what your bank would charge for a similar line of credit. American Express is one company that offers such a small-business line of credit.

Tapping into the equity in your home might be a possible way to secure funding. Banks now offer up to 125 percent equity loans. Just remember that your house is the collateral for the loan, and if the business doesn't do well and you can't make the payments, you could lose your home. Check with an accountant before getting your hopes up of using such a loan to start up the business because there are fairly tight restrictions on how you can use home equity funds. You don't want to break the rules, either inadvertently or on purpose, both because the bank could call in the whole loan if you're thought to be using the funds in an unapproved way, and because Uncle Sam is watching.

Do-It-Yourself Financing

Even with all the traditional financing options out there, some newly established lawn care and landscaping business owners prefer to use creative financing methods instead. Lowell Pitser in Stanwood, Washington, used windfalls like income tax refunds to get started. Nathan Bowers in Sykesville, Maryland, whipped out his plastic to buy the machinery, staplers, and other goodies that make the business go, then secured a vehicle loan to pay for his truck.

When using personal credit cards, watch your expenses closely. You can easily put yourself thousands of dollars in debt if you're not careful. Start out with the bare essentials so your business will have a chance to grow and prosper without the specter of debt hanging over it.

Unearthing the Green

As you can see from your startup worksheet—and the I&E you've been working on in this chapter—the startup costs for a lawn service or landscaping business can be quite low if you avoid the temptation to splurge on a bunch of cool power tools and start out with equipment and a vehicle you already have. For everything else, you may be able to rely on your personal savings to round out your equipment toolbox or fill up your tool shed. In fact, it's not uncommon for new lawn and landscaping business owners to launch a homebased business on just a few thousand dollars, as Mike Collins and Karen Deighton of Michigan did. Not counting their business vehicle, they spent about $6,000 to launch Celtic Lawn & Landscape, half of which went to general business liability and auto insurance. The other $3,000 paid for miscellaneous small tools, registration of the company name, website design, business cards, and stationery. You, too, can start your business on the cheap, especially if you have a home computer.

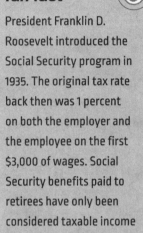

fun fact

President Franklin D. Roosevelt introduced the Social Security program in 1935. The original tax rate back then was 1 percent on both the employer and the employee on the first $3,000 of wages. Social Security benefits paid to retirees have only been considered taxable income since 1983.

If you decide to use personal savings to launch your business, make sure you have enough money in an accessible account to cover about six months of personal expenses. This is very important when you're trying to get the business off the ground because you are bound to have months when business is slow and your income will be irregular. If you're in the north, you also need to have enough cash to carry you through the winter and/or supplement any income you might make from snow plowing.

If you don't have a lot of personal savings and you need an infusion of cash to cover startup expenses and have enough of a nest egg to set your mind at ease, you may be able to obtain an unsecured personal loan from your community bank or credit union without putting up any collateral. However, as mentioned earlier, banks in general view business startups as very risky and may not be willing to give you even a little cash for that purpose. That includes home equity loans, although if you already have a line of credit established that is accessed with checks, you definitely could tap that account for business costs. Just remember, though—your home is at stake when you use a home equity loan, and you should think very carefully about whether you're willing to take that risk, even in the interest of starting your dream business.

Because traditional loans and home equity loans carry risk, it's probably better to rely on any other liquid asset you may have if you're looking for some scratch. Other sources of capital you might already have include stocks and bonds, savings bonds, certificates of deposit, and income tax refunds. Other assets, such as real estate, vehicles, and jewelry, can be sold for cash, and you could even borrow from your pension plan, IRA, 401(k) plan, SEP, or Keogh. But as with a home equity loan, tread lightly—that money is earmarked for your retirement. Should the unthinkable happen and your business doesn't succeed, your retirement will be at stake.

Some small-business owners turn to friends and family for startup funds. If you decide either to sell shares in your business or borrow outright, be sure to handle the transaction in the most professional, businesslike way possible. For instance, always sign a promissory note that details repayment terms and offers an equitable interest rate. This is particularly important if you borrow from loved ones. Nothing can destroy a tight-knit family faster than a broken promise of repayment or a misunderstanding about how it will be handled. National Family Mortgage (nationalfamilymortgage.com) is designed for loans between family members and friends. Remember how precious those relationships are. Protect them as you would any highly valuable asset.

Your Green Piece on Earth

I n Chapter 1, we mentioned with unabashed optimism all the opportunities that exist in the lawn care service industry for hard-working, dedicated, and disciplined small-business owners like you. Of course, all of these opportunities also require a stash of cash and a liberal dose of business savvy.

But for the most part, enthusiasm for the job and the tenacity to go the distance are just as crucial for success as a healthy cash infusion.

It is our hope at Entrepreneur that all your plans and hard work pay off and you enjoy both satisfaction and longevity in your newly chosen career. But even as we wish you the best as you embark on this exciting new venture, we must acknowledge that every new business owner faces pitfalls that could threaten his or her existence.

Why Businesses Fail

The reasons for business failures are numerous. Business failures in the service industry can occur due to poor customer relations, underpriced services, insufficient insurance, market conditions (such as competition, increases in the cost of doing business and so on), financing and cash flow problems, poor planning, mismanagement, and a host of other problems.

warning

The SBA reports that too many small-business owners in financial straits don't call for help until it's too late to salvage their companies. Don't fall into this trap. If you ever need help, call the SBA, which can provide advice and direction or act as a loan guarantor. There's no charge for this service, and it could save everything you've worked for.

That's why we strongly recommend that you hire professionals like attorneys, bookkeepers, accountants, and employees to assist you in the proper management and operation of your business. No matter how enthusiastic, bright, and determined you may be, you're probably not an expert in every field, and your time will only stretch so far. In the beginning, it can be pretty hard to part with the cash to pay those professional fees, but in the long run, it's worth it because this kind of help will allow you to focus your attention on the services you do and like best.

The outlook for success in your new business isn't totally grim. Statistics suggest that the longer you're in business, the better your chances are of staying afloat.

Hindsight Is 20/20

Nearly every lawn care and landscaping professional who agreed to be interviewed for this book readily admitted there were things they would do differently if it were possible to start again. For instance, Steve Mager in Mendota Heights, Minnesota, who assumed control of an established company that came complete with 60 clients, said he should have done more due diligence before agreeing to the sale. Not only did he feel he paid too much for the business, but he soon found out that the age and condition of the equipment that came along with it had been misrepresented. He solved some of his early operating problems by replacing the equipment, but "it was a hard decision to spend the dough," he says.

Nathan Bowers in Sykesville, Maryland, believes he should have paid more attention to certain business details. "A mission statement would have been extremely helpful," he admits. "I also should have created more standardized business systems so the company could have run on its own more smoothly. I think it might have helped to create a manual with specific guidelines for every aspect of the business."

Florida landscaper Mike Rosenbleeth says that finding good employees has always been his greatest challenge. "You always have to keep your ear to the ground among the people you know [because they can make referrals]," he says. "Not having employees limits how fast and how far you can grow your business."

Lowell Pitser, the Stanwood, Washington, lawn care service owner we talked to, says he wishes he had acquired the business acumen he needed sooner. He also would have liked to have started earlier in life, both because he probably could have avoided hurting his back if he was younger and because he would have been able to expand the business faster. "After eight years, I should be trying to put a third crew on instead of just now starting to put on a second crew," he says.

Another lawn service owner we know of in South Dakota believes he should have started his business earlier. He figures that by beginning while he was in his 20s rather than his late 30s, he, too, could now have multiple crews and more time to manage the business instead of going out on jobs himself. He also thinks he should have moved beyond the boundaries of his own community, where there are more than 30 lawn care companies.

Michigan landscaper Michael Collins and his business partner, Karen Deighton, would have used someone other than a friend to design their website. "We saved on the cost, but we had to keep pushing him to complete it," Collins says. "Our website isn't terrible, but I'd like something different that is both nice and professional."

Although there are things they could have done better, each of these intrepid entrepreneurs relied on

fun fact

According to Google Trends, the U.S. city with the most searches for "snow removal services" in 2010 was Minneapolis, Minnesota; in 2015, it was Chicago. The top three cities searching for the terms "lawn care services" in 2015 were Minneapolis, Minnesota; Atlanta, Georgia; and Charlotte, North Carolina. While it's not definitive to what end those searches were done, chances are good that users were searching for service providers.

creative thinking, hard work, and good, old-fashioned determination to meet challenges. Obviously, this is a strategy that works. These small-business owners not only survived that scary first year; many are prospering now.

Was it a miracle that they persevered in the face of economic uncertainties, weathering setbacks, and other pressures? Definitely not. It's due more to having the right stuff and knowing how to use it. It's also due to being willing to "go the extra mile" and provide exceptional customer service.

"I have a whole collection of notes from customers thanking me because their lawn is so beautiful," Pitser says. "There's a lot of personal satisfaction in this business because I have the immediate reward of seeing my work when it's done. I like knowing my customers are going to come home and go, 'Wow!'"

stat fact

Horticulturist Russell Nagata, Ph.D., developed a new breed of St. Augustine grass called Captiva, which grows one and a half to two and a half inches per week, half the length of typical grasses in use today that grow three to five inches per week. Its deep green color, less mowing needs, and resistance to certain bugs make it a development to watch in coming years.

All in a Day's Work

Customers aren't the only ones who say "wow" in this business. Sometimes, the owners themselves are confronted with unexpected situations that leave them shaking their heads.

Making the Grade

Part-time lawn business owner Bill Van Cleave in Urbana, Illinois, once had a close encounter of the absurd kind when he was mowing on a slope. While riding his Dixon Zero Turning Radius mower, which has a rear-mount engine, he misjudged the steepness of the slope and accidentally popped a wheelie.

"The mower got stuck in the ground with the blades in operation and me still on it," Van Cleave says. "I had to turn off the blades and the mower before I could slide over the seat and get off. Since then, I only push-mow that slope!"

Going for a Ride

One of Minnesota lawn care owner Steve Mager's employees had a similar experience with a lawn mower. Without his knowledge, someone disabled the safety feature on the mower

▶ The Signs of Success

You now know about the red flags that can signal a business failure. So what are the signs that your lawn care or landscaping business will be successful?

- ▶ You are providing a useful service at a price the market can bear.
- ▶ Your local business market has enough customers to support your business.
- ▶ You have enough savings or financing to weather the initial make-or-break period.
- ▶ Your business and marketing plans are sound, and you know where to go if you need help implementing them.
- ▶ You have a good team of supporters, including business advisors and family members.
- ▶ Your top priority is providing great customer service.
- ▶ You keep careful records and always know where your business stands financially.
- ▶ You're always aware of what your competition is up to.
- ▶ You're flexible enough to change your business strategy when the situation warrants it.
- ▶ You truly love your job and can't imagine doing anything else.

that causes it to quit running when the handle is squeezed. He was busily mowing a strip of grass in the intersection of a busy street when he squeezed the handle—and nothing happened. Because there was so much traffic, he knew he couldn't let go of the mower, so he hung on with one hand, lost his balance, and found himself being dragged behind it in ever-widening circles on the patch of grass. His heroic action no doubt prevented a serious traffic accident, and he survived the incident himself with no more than a bruised ego when his crewmate rescued him and stopped the mower.

House Call

One reason some lawn and landscaping service entrepreneurs get into the business is because they enjoy the great outdoors. One of Nathan Bowers' employees took this appreciation for nature to new heights when he was mowing around a pool one day. "Suddenly, he grabbed one of those nets you use to fish stuff out of the pool and rescued a baby rabbit from the water," Bowers says. "He even did CPR on it."

The heroic gesture worked—the bunny survived none the worse for wear and Bowers' employee nonchalantly went back to mowing.

Your Formula for Success

It's easy to see that the kind of resourcefulness and flexibility exhibited by the owners mentioned here and throughout this book are the hallmarks of lawn service and landscaping professionals. It's also worth repeating that hard work and single-minded determination are other traits these owner/operators share that have contributed to their success.

Now it's time for you to turn green grass into cold cash. Best of luck in your new venture!

Lawn Care/ Landscaping Resources

They say you can never be rich enough or thin enough. While these could be argued, we believe you can never have enough resources. Therefore, we're giving you a wealth of sources to check into, check out, and harness for your own personal information blitz.

These sources are tidbits—ideas to get you started on your research. They are by no means the only sources out there, and they should not be taken as the ultimate answer. We have done our research and rechecked all for this update, but businesses do tend to move, change, fold, and expand without notice. As we have repeatedly stressed, do your homework. Get out there and start investigating!

Advertising Specialty Items and Opportunities

Big Promotions, (214) 295-5946, www.bigpromotions.net

Blueberry Ink, (800) 837-0337, www.blueberryink.com

Gaebler Ventures, (312) 267-0060, www.gaebler.com

Specialty Promotions Unlimited, (phone orders discouraged), www.specprom.com

Yelp, (877) 767-9357, www.yelp.com/business

Attorney Referrals

American Bar Association, Service Center (800) 285-2221, www.americanbar.org

Martindale.com, (800) 526-4902, www.martindale.com

Demographic Information

American Demographics, The AdAge Group, www.adage.com

U.S. Census Bureau, www.census.gov

City Data, www.city-data.com

Employee Assistance

U.S. Department of Labor, www.dol.gov

Estimating Books

The Complete Business Manual for Landscape Irrigation & Maintenance Contractors, Charles Vander Kooi, Vander Kooi & Associates (1996)

Landscape Estimating & Contract Administration, Stephen Angley, Edward Horsey and David Roberts, Delmar Cenage Learning (2001)

Landscape Estimating Methods, Sylvia Hollman Fee, R.S. Means Company (2007)

Franchise Opportunities

Clean Air Lawn Care, http://cleanairlawncare.com

Lawn Doctor, Inc., (800) 989-1903, http://lawndoctorfranchise.com, jasonbarclay@ lawndoctor.com

NaturaLawn of America, (800) 989-5444, www.naturallawn.com, info@naturallawn.com

NiteLites Outdoor Lighting Franchise, (866) NITELITES, www.nitelites.com

Outdoor Lighting Perspectives, (888) 308-7138, www.outdoorlightingfranchise.com

Spray Green Landscape Service, (888) 59GREEN, www.spraygreen.net

Spring-Green Lawn Care, www.spring-green.com

U.S. Lawns, (800) US-LAWNS, http://uslawns.com

Weed Man, (888) 321-WEED, www.weedmanfranchise.com

Graphic Design Services

Green Industry Marketing Consultants, Focal Point Communications (800) 525-6999, www.growpro.com

Green Industry Websites

http://AthleticTurf.net

www.LandscapeManagement.net

www.LandscapingNetwork.com

www.LawnSite.com

www.ProGardenBiz.com

www.TurfTrends.com

Home and Garden Publications

Better Homes and Gardens, Meredith Corporation (800) 374-4244, www.bhg.com/ service

Garden Guide, www.gardenguides.com

Home and Garden Shows

Buffalo Home & Garden Show, (716) 429-6626, www.buffalohomeshow.com

Capital Home Show, (888) 248-9751, www.capitalhomeshow.com

Cleveland Home & Garden Show, (440) 248-5729, www.greatbighomeandgarden.com

Dayton Home & Garden Show, HSI Show Productions (800) 215-1700, www.daytonhgs.com

Green Industry and Equipment Expo, (800) 558-8767, www.gie-expo.com

Minneapolis Home & Garden Show, (952) 933-3850, www.homeandgardenshow.com

Oklahoma City Home & Garden Show, (800) 395-1350, www.oklahomacityhomeshow.com

Spring Home and Garden Show, Building Industry Association of Southeastern Michigan (313) 600-5812, www.novihomeshow.com

Texas Home & Garden Show, (713) 874-2231, http://texashomeandgarden.com

Lawn and Landscape Industry Conferences and Trade Shows

Agronomy Day, University of Illinois, College of Agriculture, (217) 333-340, http://agronomyday.cropsci.illinois.edu

Central Environmental Nursery, Trade Show (CENTS), The Ohio Nursery and Landscape Association, (800) 825-5062, www.onla.org

GIE + EXPO, GIE Media, Inc., (800) 558-8767, www.gie-expo.com info@gie-expo.com

Snow Magazine Inner Circle, GIE Media, Inc., (800) 456-0707, www.snowmagazineonline.com

Heartland Green Industry Expo, Heart of America Golf Course Superintendents Association, (816) 561-5323, www.hagcsa.org

iLandscape Show, (800) 223-8761, www.ilandscapeshow.com, information@ilca.net

The Landscape Show, Florida Nursery, Growers, and Landscape Association, (800) 375-3642, www.fngla.org, info@fngla.org

Lawn and Landscape Industry Trade Publications

Irrigation & Green Industry Newsletter (818) 342-3204, www.igin.com, info@igin.com

Landscape Architect and Specifier News, Landscape Communications, Inc., (714) 979-5276, http://landscapearchitect.epubxp.com. Subscriptions available at www.landscapeonline.com

Lawn & Landscape magazine, (800) 456-0707, www.lawnandlandscape.com

Turf magazine, Grand View Media, (802) 748-8908, www.turfmagazine.com

Landscape Contractor, Landscape Communications, Inc., (714) 979-5276, http://landscapecontractor.epubxp.com

Landscape Management

Landscape Superintendent and Maintenance Professional, www.landscapeonline.com

ProGardenBiz, www.progardenbiz.com

Green Industry Pros, www.greenindustrypros.com

Landscape Management, North Coast Media, (216) 706-3700, http://landscapemanagement.net

Golfdom (including Turfgrass Trends), North Coast Media, (216) 706-3700, www.golfdom.com

Water Garden News, BowTie, Inc., (949) 855-8822, www.mcnews.com/wgn/home.aspx

Lawn Care Equipment Manufacturers and Resale Venues

American Honda Motor Co., Inc., http://hondapowerequipment.com

eBay, www.ebay.com

Exmark Manufacturing Co., Inc., www.exmark.com

Farmers Exchange, (931) 433-9737, https://farmersexchange.com

John Deere, www.deere.com

RedMax, Husqvarna Group, www.redmax.com

Scag Power Equipment, Division of Metalcraft of Mayville, Inc., www.scag.com

Snapper, Inc., Briggs and Stratton Power Products Group, LLC, www.snapper.com, info@snapper.com

Stihl, Inc., (800) GO-STIHL, www.stihlusa.com

The Toro Company, (888) 552-5153, www.toro.com

Logo Design, Promotional Materials, and Printing

BusinessLogo.net, (888) 352-5646, www.businesslogo.net

Modern Postcard, (800) 959-8365, www.modernpostcard.com

Vistaprint, www.vistaprint.com

123 Print, (800) 877-5147, www.123print.com

Magnets on the Cheap, (877) 419-6766, www.magnetsonthecheap.com

Wholesale Magnetic Signs, (866) 769-SIGN, www.wholesalemagneticsigns.com

OC Signs, Quick Signs, (866) 267-4467, www.ocsigns.com, sales@ocsigns.com

Merchant Accounts and eCommerce Solutions

Total Merchant Services, Inc., (888) 848-6825 ext. 9420, www.totalmerchantservices.com

InfoMerchant, Infofaq, LLC, www.infomerchant.net

Square, https://squareup.com

TransFirst (Wells Fargo), www.transfirst.com

Office Supplies, Forms, and Stationery

Amsterdam Printing, (800) 203-9917, www.amsterdamprinting.com, customerservice@amsterdamprinting.com

Deluxe, (800) 865-1913, www.deluxe.com

Office Depot, (800) GO-DEPOT, www.officedepot.com

Paper Direct, (800) 272-7377, www.paperdirect.com

Rapidforms, (800) 257-8354, www.rapidforms.com, service@rapidforms.com

Staples, (800) 782-7537, www.staples.com

Point-of-Sale Software and Hardware

International Point of Sale, (866) 468-5767, www.internationalpointofsale.com, sales@internationalpointofsale.com

POSMicro, (800) 241-6264, http://posmicro.com, service@posmicro.com

First Data, (800) 538-0651, www.firstdata.com, paymentsoftware.support@firstdata.com

Printing Resources

48hourprint.com, (800) 844-0599, www.48hourprint.com

ColorPrintingCentral, (800) 309-3291, www.colorprintingcentral.com

Door Hangers.com, (704) 430-8242, www.doorhangers.com

Focal Point Communications, (800) 525-6999, www.growpro.com

Print Industry Exchange, LLC, (703) 631-4533, www.printindustry.com, info@printindustry.com

Printing for Less, (800) 930-6040, www.printingforless.com, info@printingforless.com

PSPrint, (800) 511-2009, www.psprint.com

Professional Employer Organization Information

National Association of Professional Employer Organizations, (703) 836-0466, www.napeo.org, info@napeo.org

Professional Lawn and Landscape Associations

American Horticulture Society, (800) 777-7931, www.ahs.org

AmericanHort, (202) 789-2900, www.americanhort.org

American Society of Landscape Architects, (202) 898-2444, www.asla.org

Association of Professional Landscape Designers, (717) 238-9780, www.apld.org

California Landscape Contractors Association, (916) 830-2780, www.clca.org

Independent Turf and Ornamental Distributors Association, (877) 326-5995, www.itoda.org, info@itoda.org

The Irrigation Association, (703) 536-7080, www.irrigation.org, info@irrigation.org

Landscape Maintenance Association, (941) 714-0459, www.floridalma.org, Lmaflorida@aol.com

National Association of Landscape Professionals, (703) 736-9666, www.
   landscapeprofessionals.org

National Gardening Association, (802) 863-5251, www.garden.org

North American Rock Garden Society, www.nargs.org

Outdoor Power Equipment and Engine Service Association, (860) 767-1770,
   www.opeesa.com

Professional Grounds Management Society, (410) 223-2861, www.pgms.org

Sports Turf Managers Association, (800) 323-3875, www.stma.org

Turfgrass Producers International, (800) 405-8873, www.turfgrasssod.org

Safety Equipment and Information

Tool Dudes, LLC, (877) 986-6538, www.contractorstools.com

Occupational Safety and Health Administration (OSHA), (800) 321-OSHA, www.osha.
   gov

Snow Removal Equipment

Bonnell Industries, Inc., Used Equipment Division, (800) 851-9664, www.
   bonnellusedequipment.com

U.S. Municipal, (800) 222-1980, www.usmuni.com

Software

CLIP, Sensible Software, Inc., (301) 874-3611, www.clip.com

DynaSCAPE, Garden Graphics, (800) 710-1900, www.dynascape.com

GardenSoft, (805) 492-0120, www.gardensoft.com

GroundsKeeper Pro, Adkad Technologies (800) 586-4683, www.adkad.com

LandPro, LandPro Systems, www.landprosystems.com, management@cjfiore.com

Pro Contractor Studio, Software Republic (936) 372-9884, www.softwarerepublic.com/pcs/

Sage 50, (877) 291-8401, www.sage.com/us/sage-50-accounting

PRO Landscape, Drafix Software, Inc., (816) 842-4955, http://prolandscape.com

QuickBooks, Intuit, Inc., (888) 729-1996, http://quickbooks.intuit.com

Real Green Systems, (888) 345-2154, www.realgreen.com

Successful Lawn Care/Landscaping Business Owners

Clean Air Lawn Care, Kelly Giard (888) 969-3669, www.cleanairlawncare.com, moose@cleanairlawncare.com

Greenwise Organic Lawn Care, LLC, Marc Wise and Lindsay Stame (224) 577-9473, www.iamgreenwise.com, info@iamgreenwise.com

The Cutting Crew, Steve Mager (651) 456-9771

Premier Lawn Services, Inc., Nathan Bowers, (410) 531-1147

Tax Advice and Software

Intuit TurboTax for Business, (800) 440-3279, https://turbotax.intuit.com

IRS, (800) 829-1040, www.irs.gov

Technical Assistance with Electronic Devices

Geek Squad, (800) 433-5778, www.geeksquad.com

Trailers

All Pro, (800) 622-7003, www.trailersuperstore.com

Tiger Trailers, Inc., (903) 577-9511, www.tigertrailersinc.com

Low Price Trailers of San Antonio, (210) 822-0574, www.lowpricetrailerssanantonio.com

R and P Carriages, (815) 357-3292, www.needatrailer.com

Turfgrass Management/Landscape Design Courses

Auburn University, College of Agriculture, www.agriculture.auburn.edu

Clemson University, Landscape Architecture Programs, (864) 656-3926, www.clemson.edu/caah/departments/la/

Colorado State University, CSU Turfgrass, http://csuturf.colostate.edu/Pages/extension.htm

Columbia University School of Professional Studies, (212) 854-9666, www.ce.columbia.edu/landscape

Cornell University, Soil and Crop Sciences Section, https://scs.cals.cornell.edu

Michigan State University, College of Agriculture and Natural Resources, www.canr.msu.edu/majors/crop_and_soil_sciences

Michigan State University, School of Planning, Design and Construction: Landscape Architecture, (517) 432-0704, www.spdc.msu.edu

Ohio State University, Turfgrass Science Program, Department of Horticulture and Crop Science (614) 292-1809, http://hcs.osu.edu/, randle.15@osu.edu

Penn State University, Center for Turfgrass Science, http://plantscience.psu.edu/research/centers/turf, pjl1@psu.edu

Texas A&M University, College of Agriculture and Life Sciences, http://aglifesciences.tamu.edu/

University of California–Berkeley, Department of Landscape Architecture and Environmental Planning, http://ced.berkeley.edu/academics/landscape-architecture-environmental-planning

University of Florida Institute of Food and Agricultural Sciences, (305) 292-4504, http://ifas.ufl.edu/

University of Florida, Department of Landscape Architecture, (352) 392-6098, https://dcp.ufl.edu/landscape/

University of Georgia, College of Agricultural and Environmental Sciences, www.caes.uga.edu

University of Illinois at Urbana-Champaign, Department of Landscape Architecture (217) 333-0176, www.landarch.uiuc.edu, ladept@illinois.edu

University of Kentucky, College of Agriculture, Food, and Environment, (859) 257-2000, www.uky.edu/Ag/ukturf

Web Hosting

Domain.com, www.domain.com

AT&T Web Hosting, www.webhosting.att.com

Work Shirts and Hats

Deluxe, (800) 865-1913, www.deluxe.com

Lids (888) 564-4287, www.lids.com

Glossary

Aerating: loosening or puncturing the soil to increase water penetration and air permeability, which improves plant growth

Annual: a plant started from seed that lives for just one season

Arbor: a type of shade structure (usually wooden) that extends off a house to provide shade

Balancing weight: an inexpensive weight used on a lawn mower to help prolong mower life

Bedline: a demarcation line between the planting areas and the lawn

Bubble diagram: a landscaping plan that is drawn using circles on a base map to indicate proposed locations of features like flower beds, deck, patio, etc.

CAD: computer-aided design

Clip art: simple graphics like drawings, photographs, and other artwork that can be inserted into documents; Microsoft Word and other word processing programs come with a small clip art collection as part of the main program

Contingency fee: payment for legal services rendered as a percentage of a settlement amount (often 25 percent or higher)

Curtain drain: a trench with perforated pipe set in a gravel bed and covered with soil to carry water away from structures or low spots

Dba: "doing business as," refers to your adoption of a pseudonym as the name of your business that is registered with your local or state government to make sure it's unique

Deciduous: shedding at the end of a period of growth, as in trees that lose their leaves in the fall

Die cut: a hole or decorative shape cut into any type of material (including paper or cardboard); the hole at the top of a door hanger

Door hanger: an inexpensive advertising piece that can be hung on the doorknob of prospects' homes or offices

Downlighting: landscape lighting installed to provide security in open areas or to spotlight dramatic plantings

Ergonomic: designed for physical comfort and safety (i.e., an ergonomic chair)

Feng Shui: the ancient Chinese art of placement thought to improve the flow of chi, or energy, though the body

Footings: the bottom part of a wall

Freelancer: a self-employed person who works on a project or contract basis for businesses; also known as an independent contractor

French drain: a trench with perforated pipe set in gravel that carries water away from structures or low spots; differs from a curtain drain because the gravel is left exposed

Gazebo: an outdoor room without walls that is placed on a foundation and may have an electrical source and bench seating

Grading: leveling the soil to a desired height or contour

Groundcover: low-growing perennial plants that cover a large part of the ground, both for ornamental purposes and to serve as the front layer of a planting bed

Guying: stabilizing a tree with guy wires or ropes attached to ground stakes

Hardscape: the parts of a landscape that are nonliving, like rocks and bricks

Hydroseeding: a lawn seeding technique in which a watery slurry of seed, fertilizer, soil binder, and/or mulch is applied to the prepared ground

Indicia: preprinted mark in the upper right-hand corner of a piece of bulk mail that shows that postage was paid by the sender and its origin of the mailing

Independent contractor: *see* Freelancer

Litigator: an attorney who represents a client in a lawsuit

Kerf: the gap left by a saw blade when it cuts into wood

Logo (or logotype): an identifying symbol used by companies in advertising or marketing; examples of logos are John Deere's leaping stag symbol and the Detroit Tigers' English "D" with its snarling tiger

Mail merge: a computer software feature that merges a list of names and addresses into a form letter (this function is used for direct marketing and offered through word-processing programs like Word)

Measuring wheel: a handheld device for pacing and measuring the dimensions of lawns and other areas

MSDS: material safety data sheets, which are required by law for contractors who use hazardous materials such as pesticides

Pavilion: a large outdoor structure without walls usually used for enclosing a spa or entertaining

Perennial: a plant that blooms year after year, although it usually goes into dormancy during the winter months

Pergola: an outdoor structure often used to cover a passageway

pH level: a measure of acid and/or alkaline levels used for monitoring soil

Point-of-sale terminal: electronic equipment used to verify that a customer's credit is good

Poly bag: a plastic sleeve that newspaper carriers (and others who deliver printed material) use to protect the paper from getting wet in inclement weather

Portal: in internet parlance, the electronic gateway users "pass through" to access websites

Powdery mildew: a common lawn disease of bluegrass, especially in the fall; shady lawns and lawns on the north side of houses are more likely to become infected

Power raking: a technique for removing thatch and moss from lawns

Rebar: steel used to reinforce concrete in block walls and other structures

Resolution: the clarity achieved by a printer or monitor, expressed as dpi

Retainer: money paid in advance for services rendered at a later time

Rust: a common type of lawn fungus that tends to occur from mid- to late summer when the temperature soars and lawn growth slows down; it most commonly affects Kentucky bluegrass, perennial ryegrass, and tall fescue, and the orange spores can be spread from lawn to lawn

Server: the computer that controls access to a network or peripherals (such as printers and disk drives)

Silviculturist: a landscaping professional who specializes in the care of trees, especially in forests

Tag line: a slogan or block of descriptive text used to build audience recognition for a product (e.g., "Got milk?")

Softscape: the living part of the landscape (e.g., plants, lawn, trees)

Swale: a sloping surface ditch used to direct water away from a building or landscaped area

Terracing: a technique for turning sloping landscape into flat, usable garden space

Thatch: a dead layer of organic material (usually grass) that builds up between the soil and grass and can choke off water and nutrients

Topiary: a shrub or tree cut into ornamental shapes; the fanciful "yard art" the title character creates in the movie Edward Scissorhands is an example of topiaries

Uplighting: landscape lighting (typically flood lights) that dramatically light trees or other distinctive home features

White finger: a form of Raynaud's disease caused by exposure to constant vibration, impairing circulation and causing fingers and toes to throb painfully after exposure to the cold (the affected digits appear tight, white, and shiny, then turn red as they warm up—sufferers often have a reduced ability to grip objects)

Windbreak: a barrier of trees or shrubs installed to deflect harsh winds

Xeriscape: from the Greek word xeros, meaning "dry," this term refers to landscaping that is designed to conserve water

Zero turn radius: refers to a lawn mower's transaxle and its ability to turn the rear wheels independently of both the power and steering control, allowing the operator to make 360-degree turns

Index